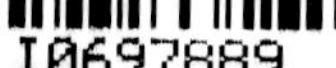

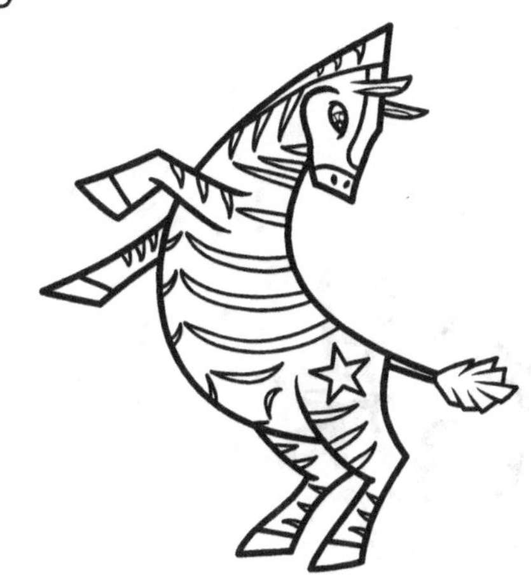
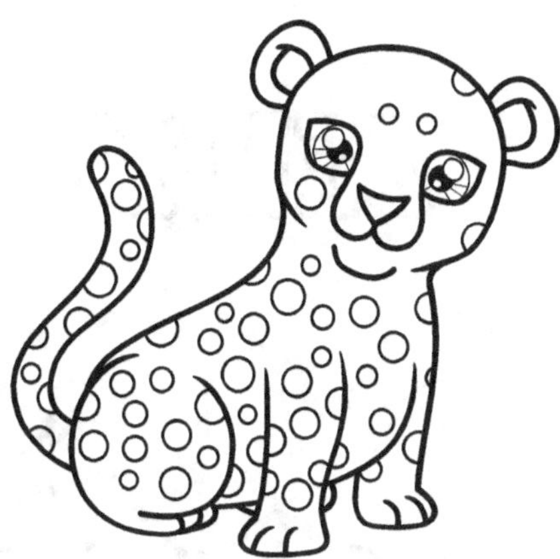

WILDLIFE
COLORING BOOK

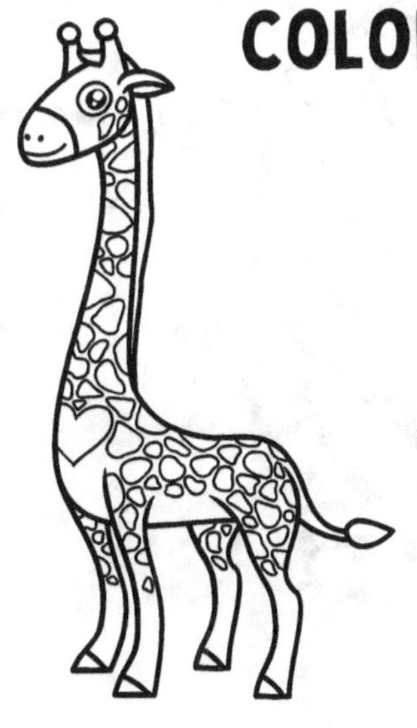
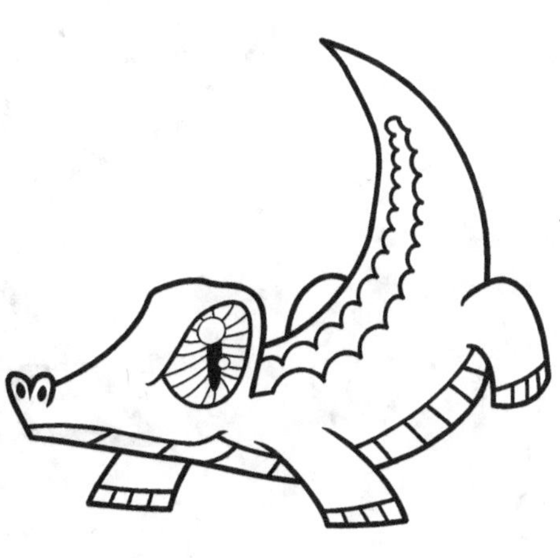

ZEBRA

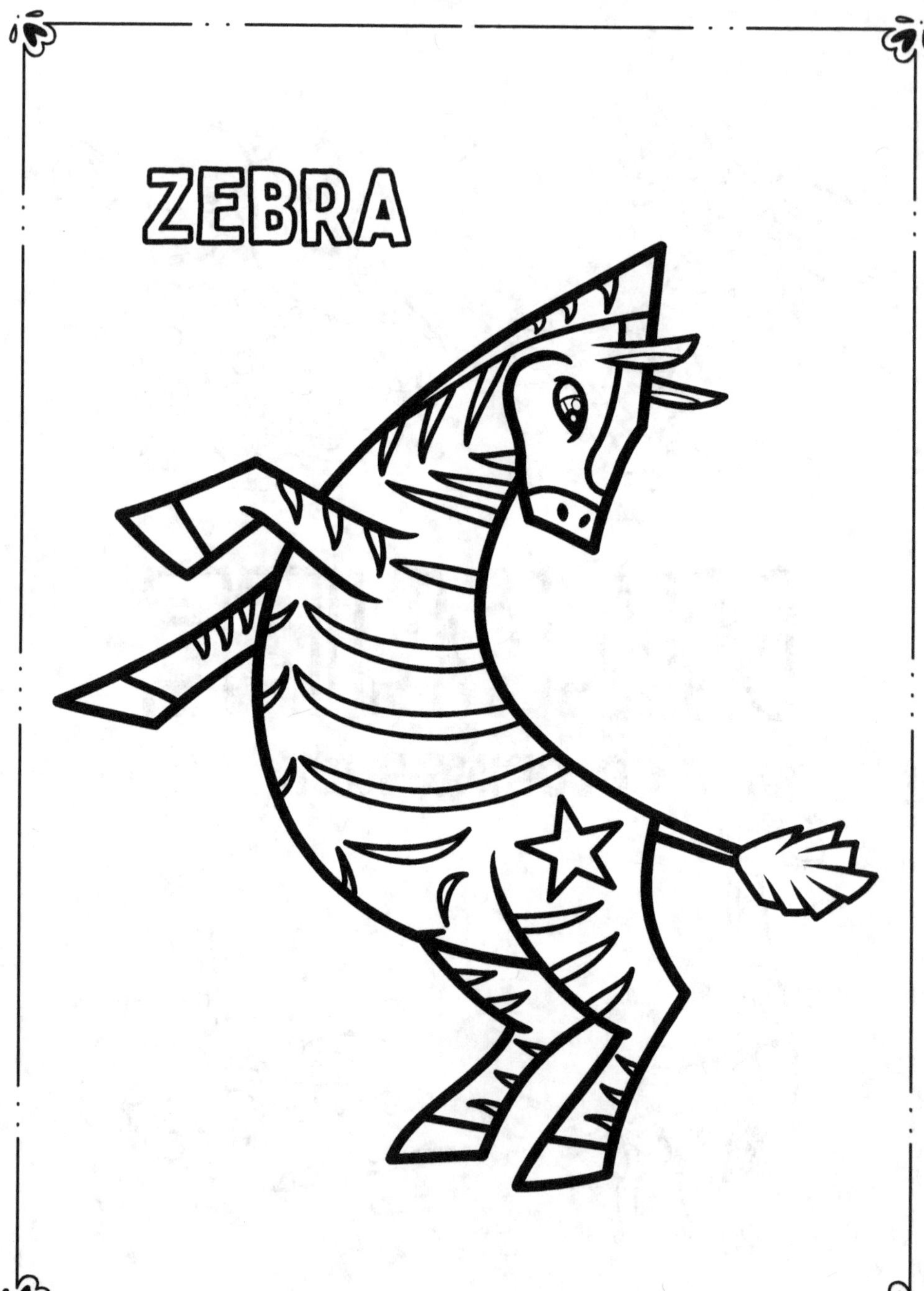

TORTOISE

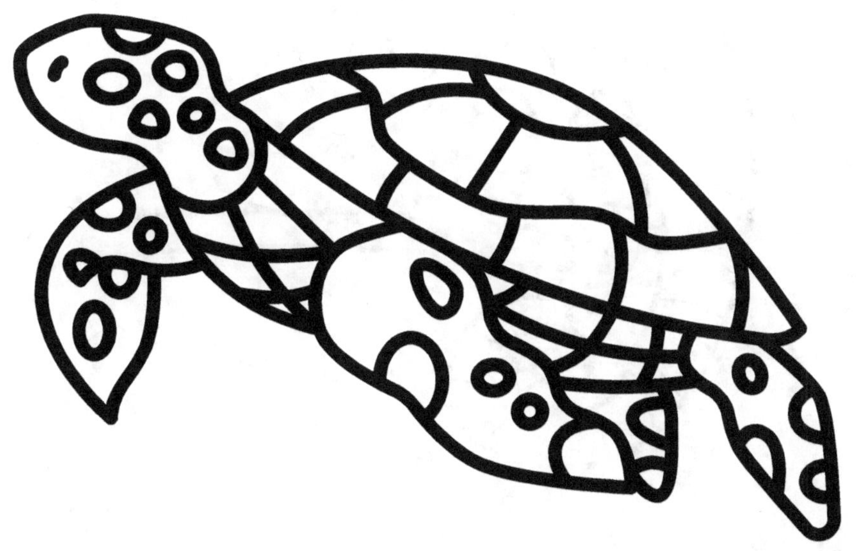

CHAMELEON

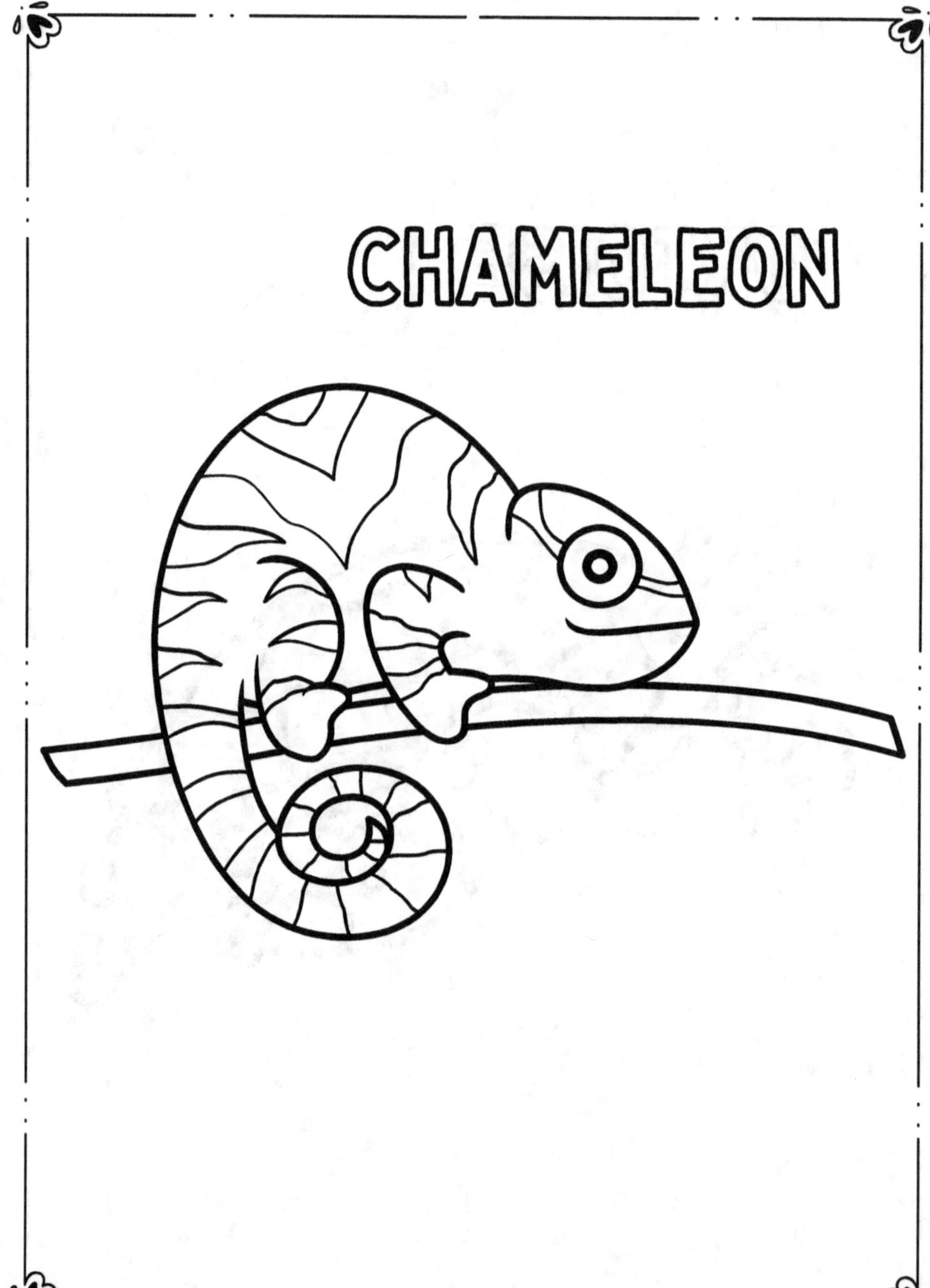

CHEETAH

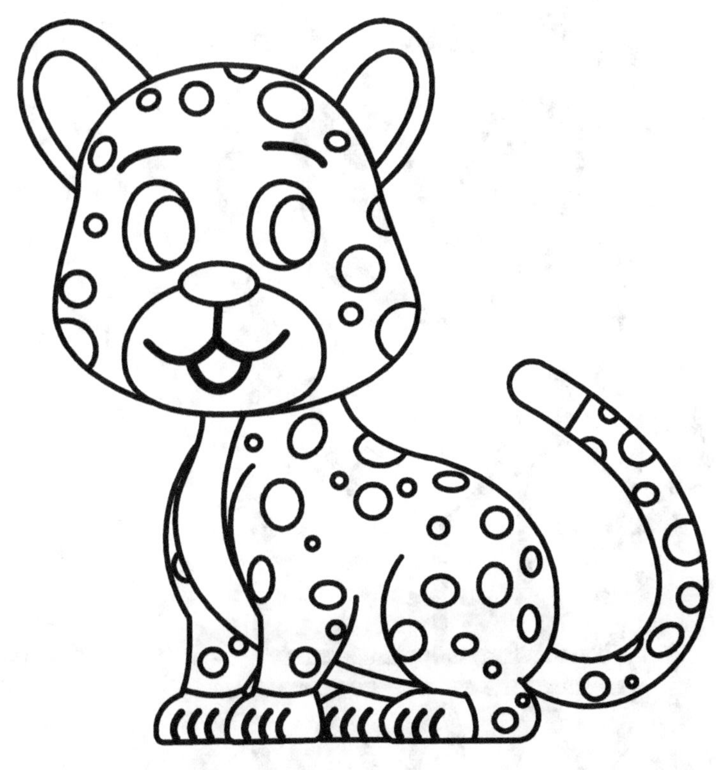

LION

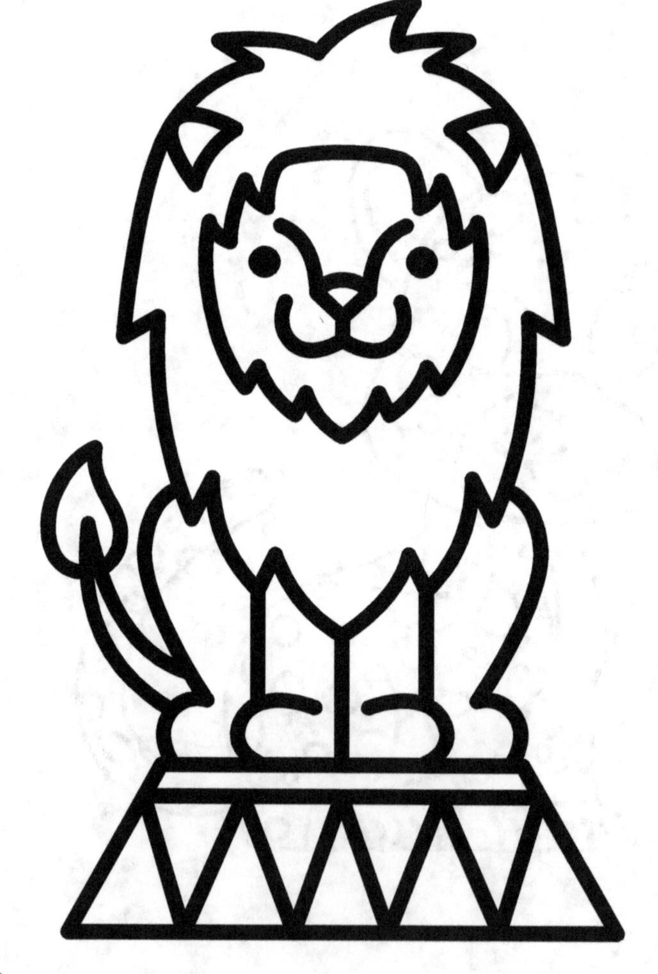

KANGAROO

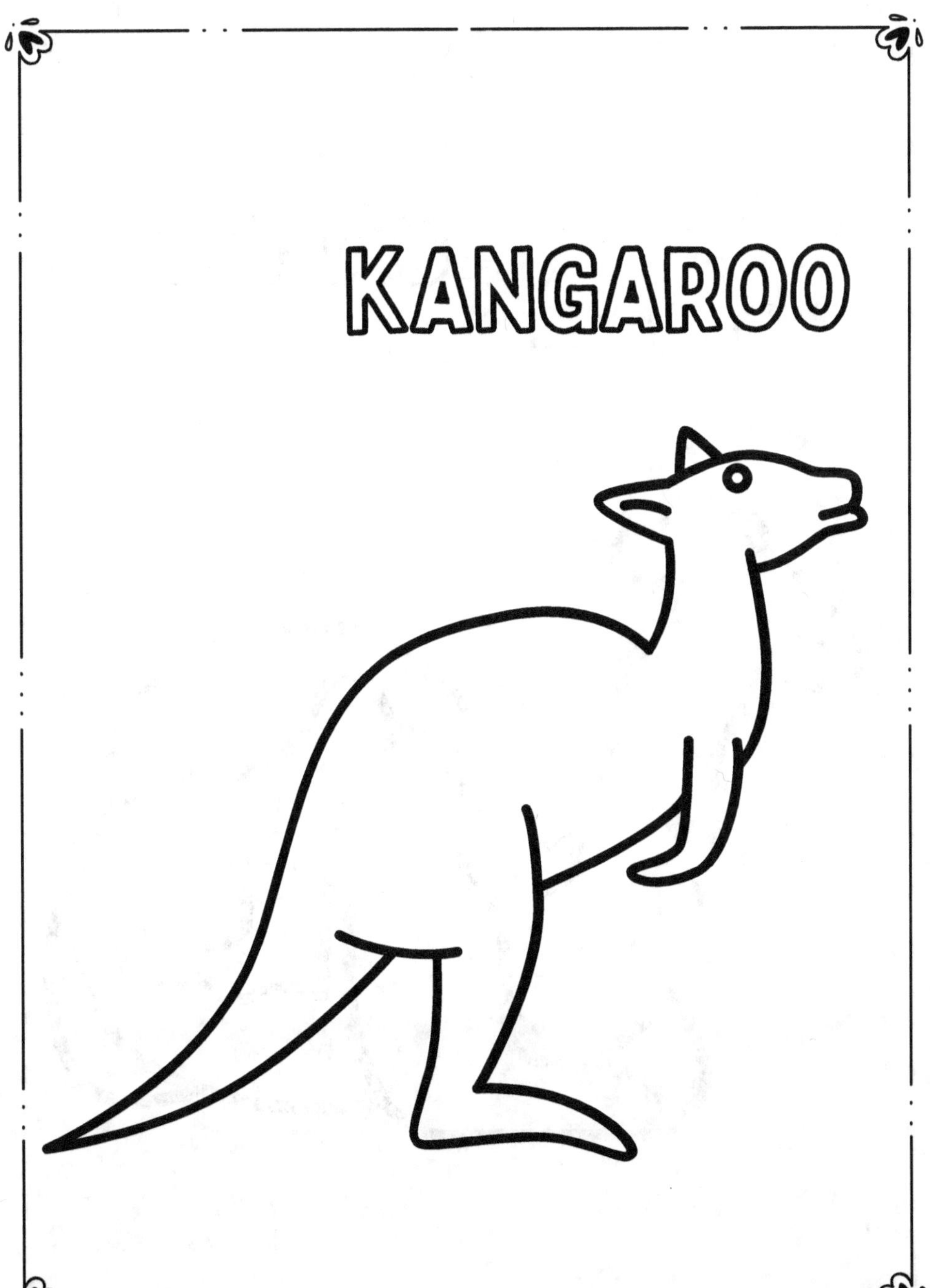

CAMEL

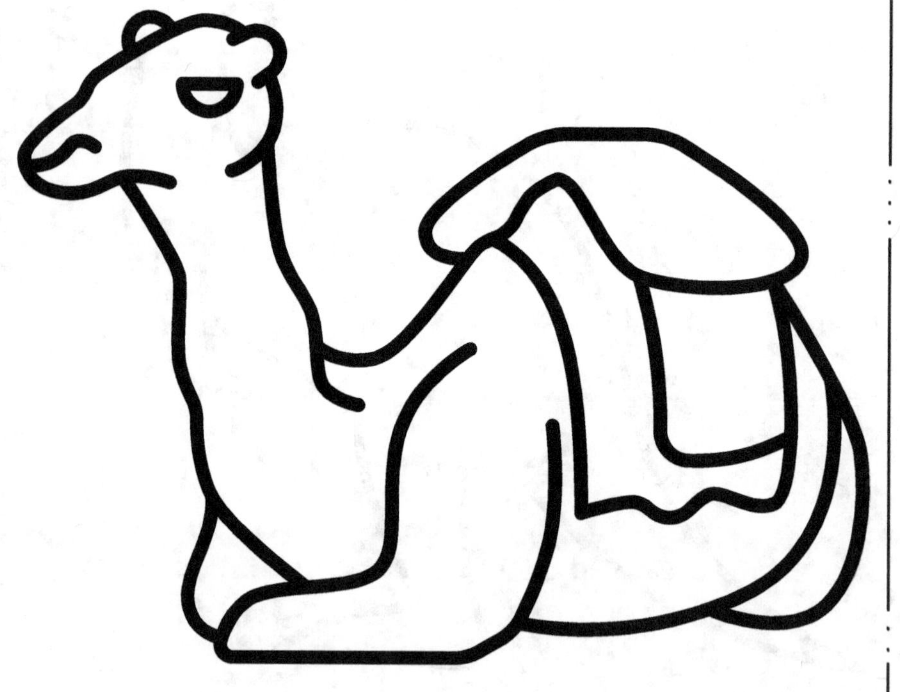

MONKEY

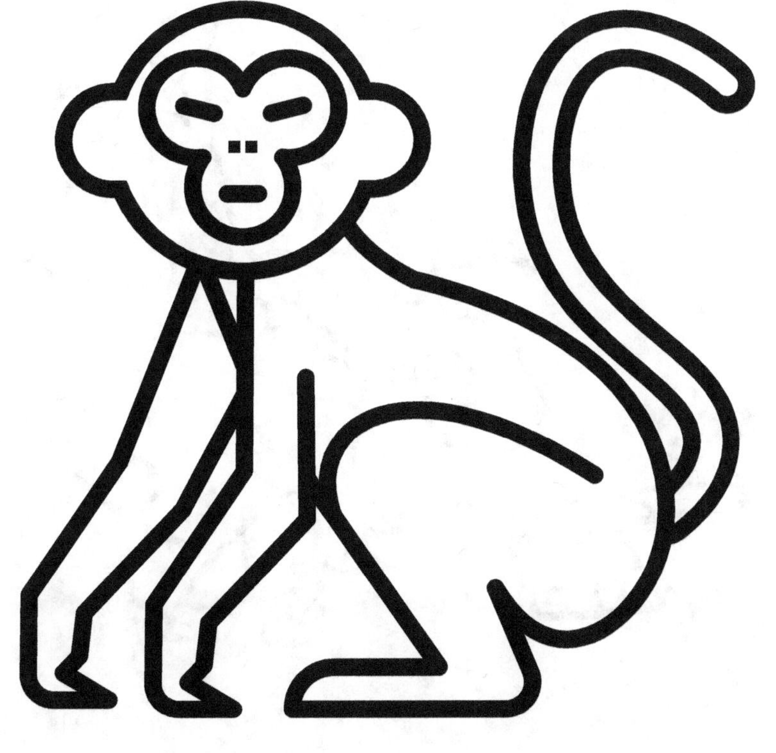

ALLIGATOR

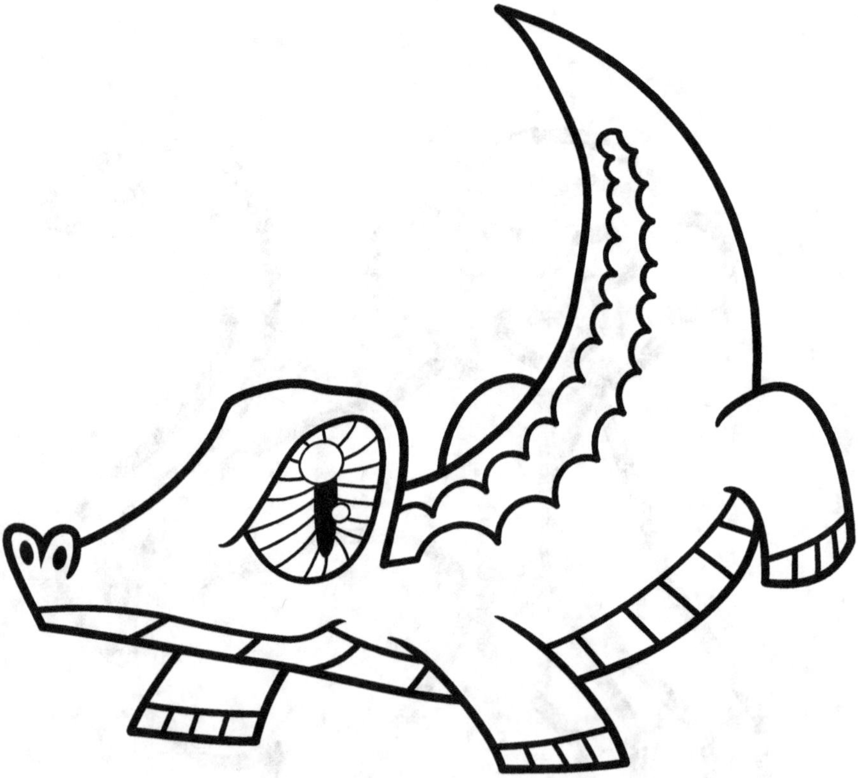

HIPPO

LIZARD

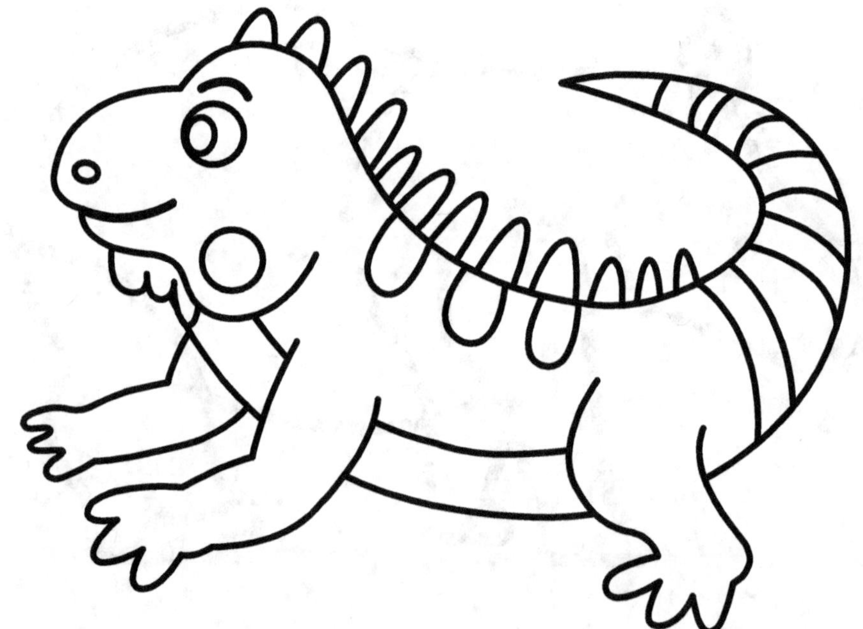

GORILLA

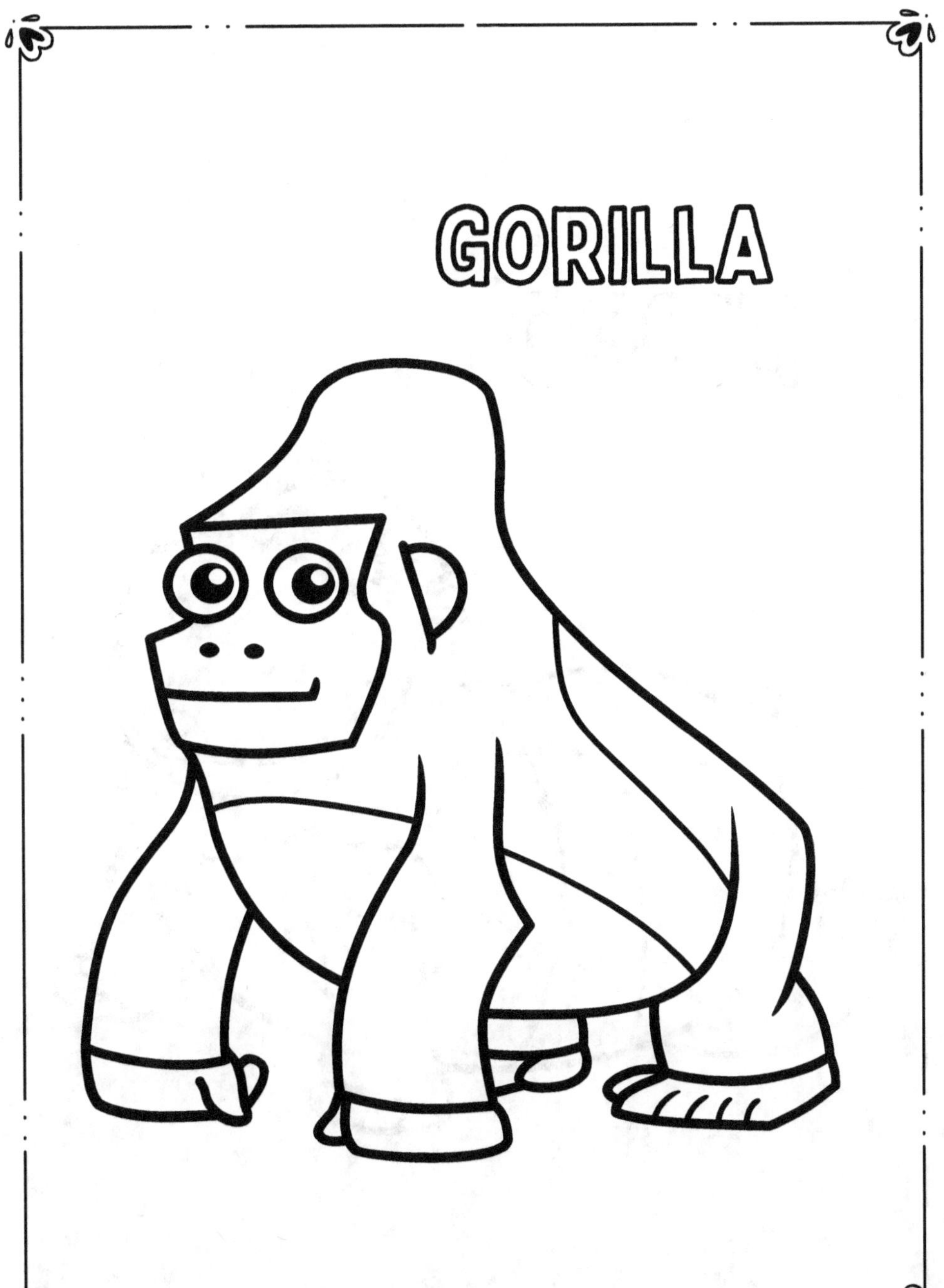

HIPPO

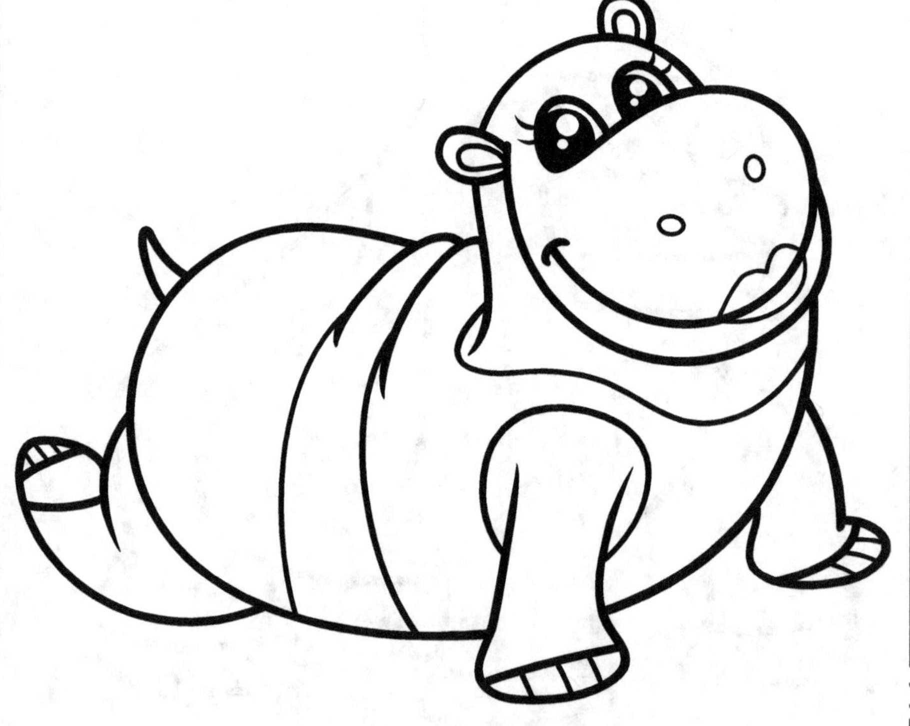

PANDA

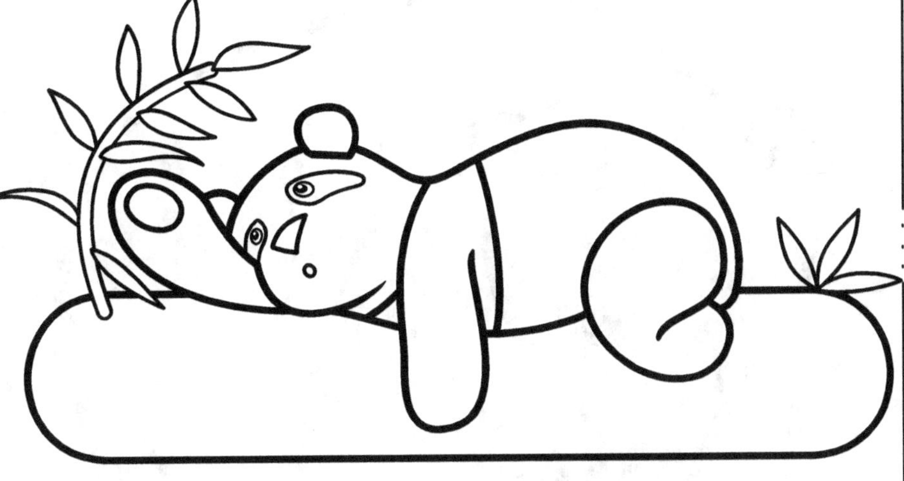

BEAR

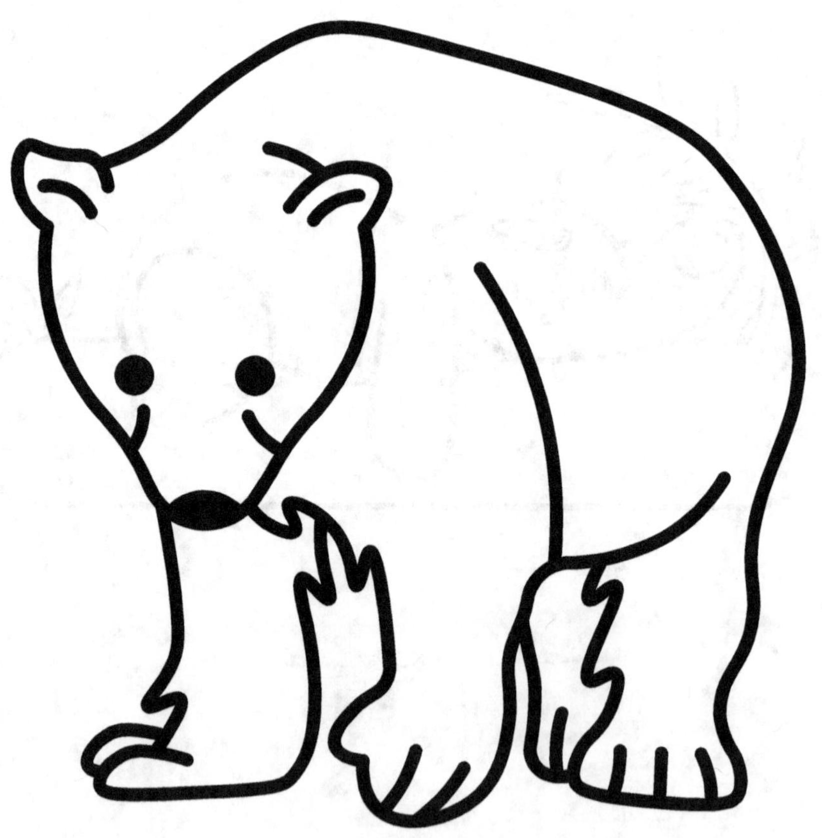

COBRA

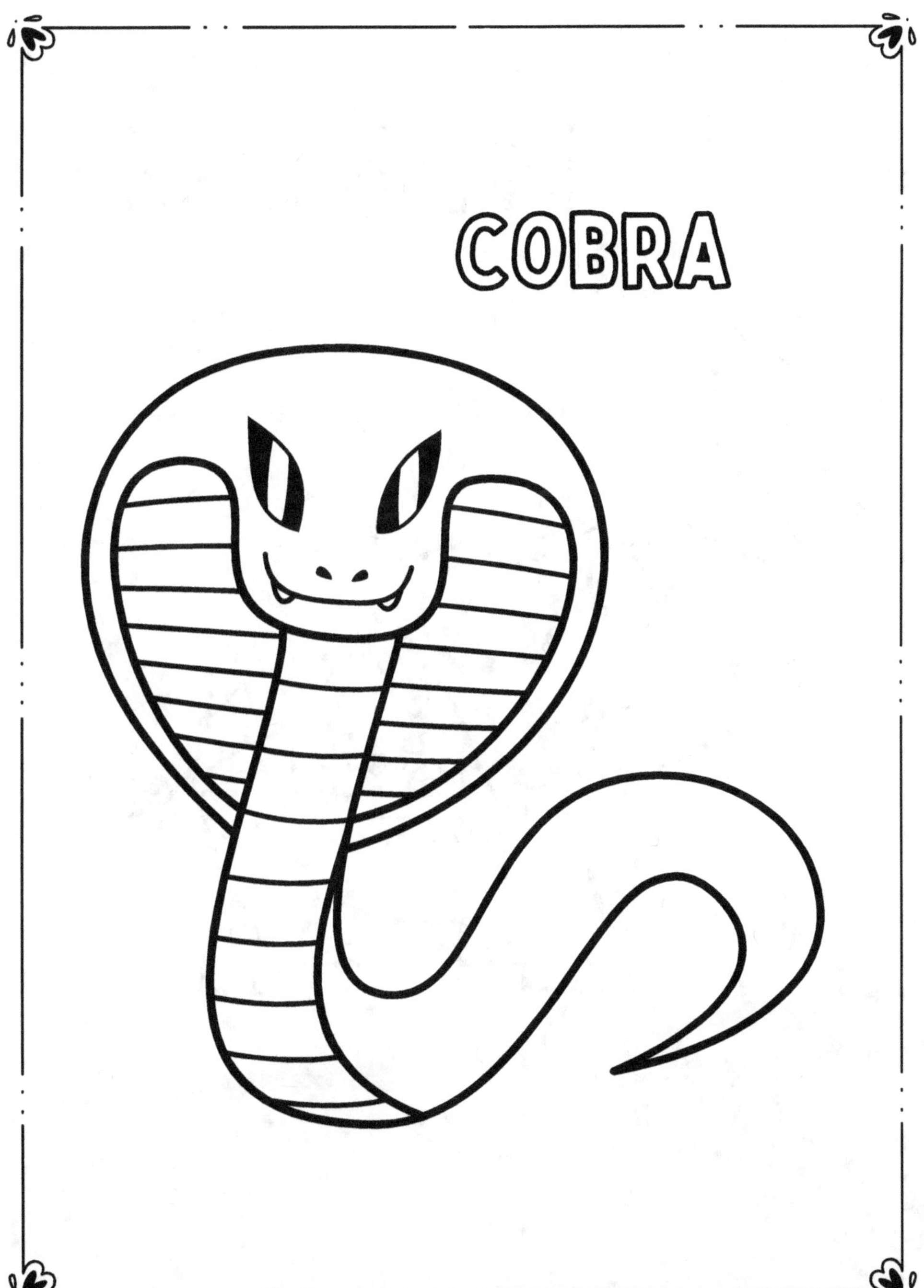

ELEPHANT

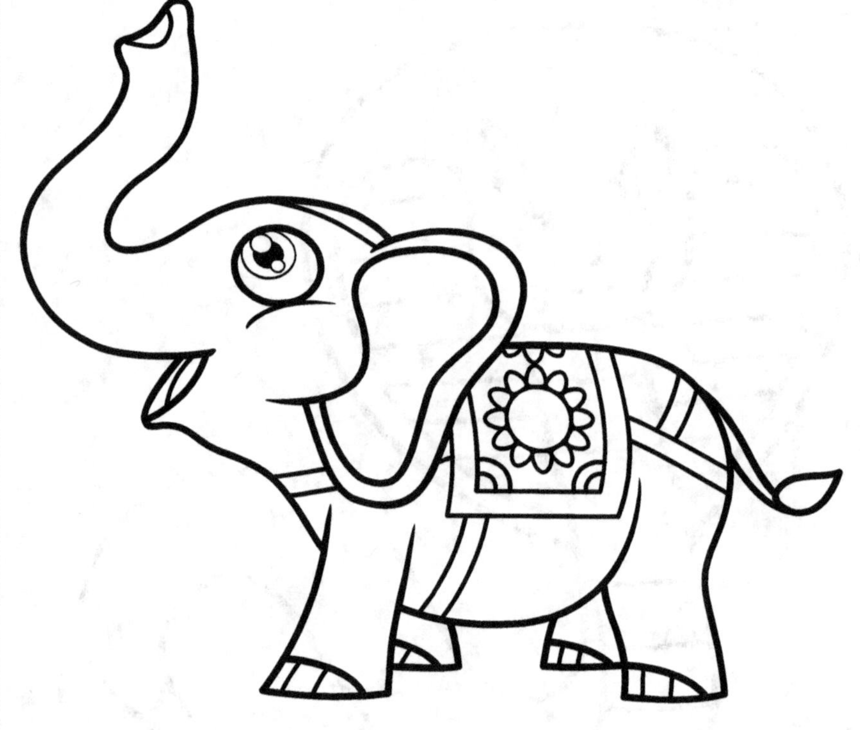

RHINO

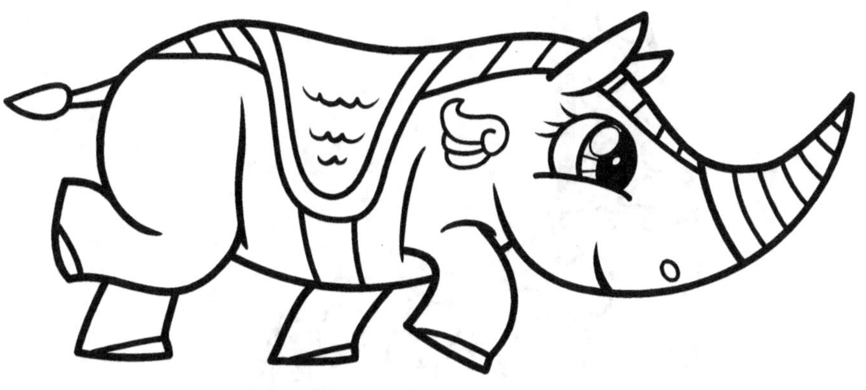

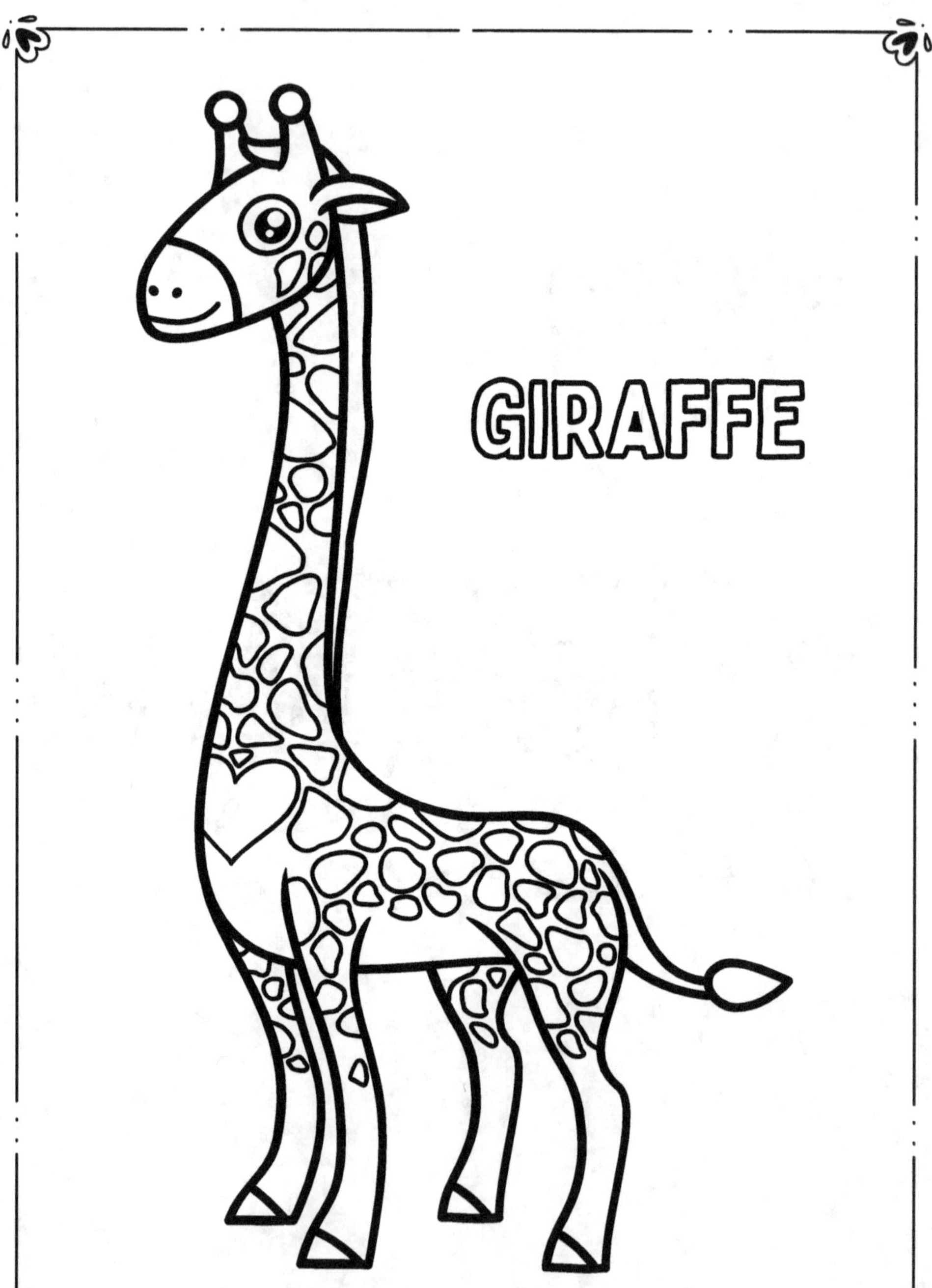

GIRAFFE

KOALA

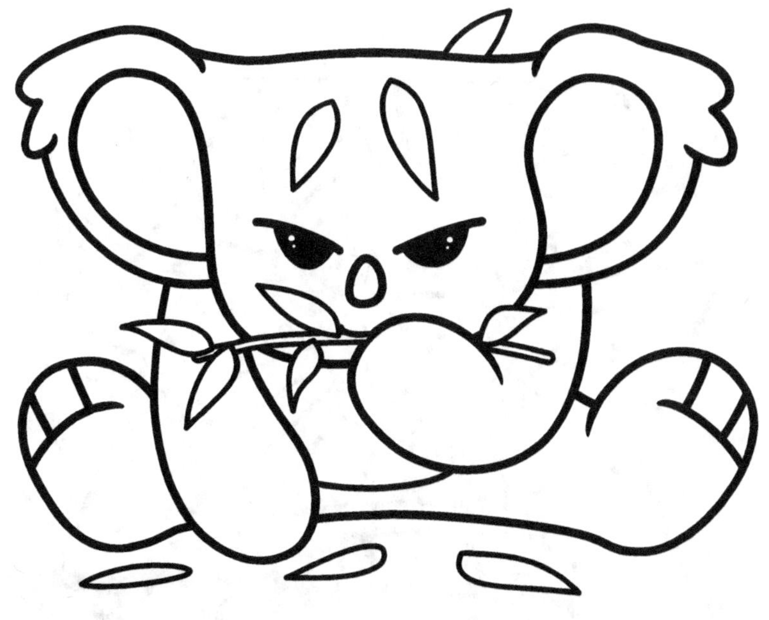

LION

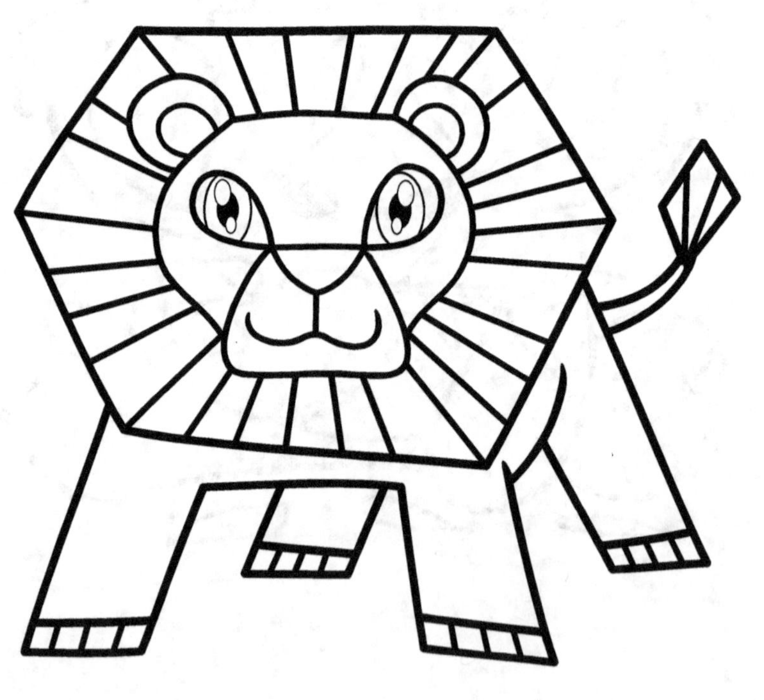

CHEETAH

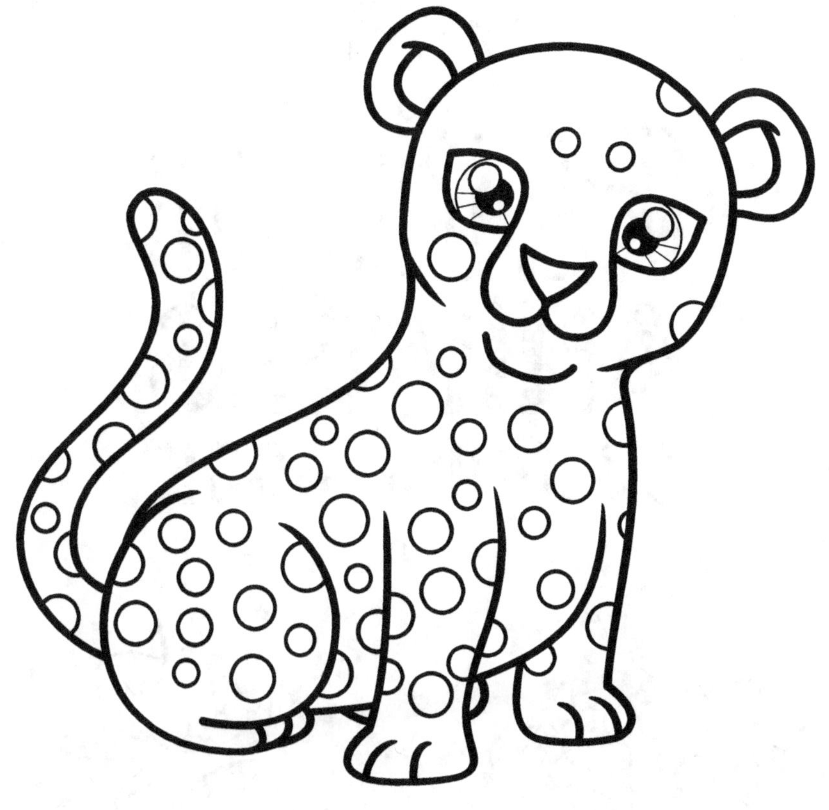

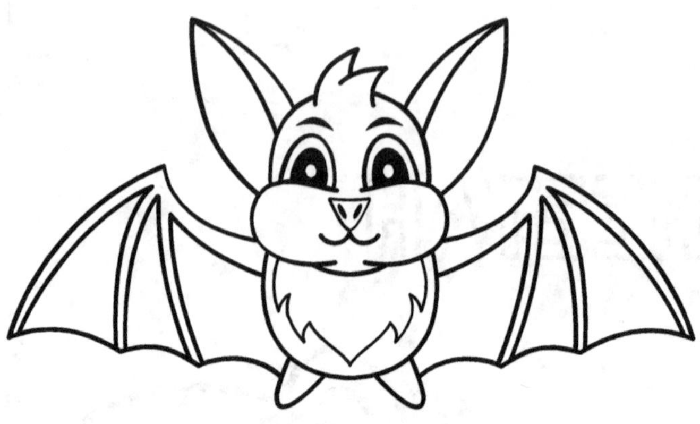

FLYING ANIMALS
COLORING BOOK

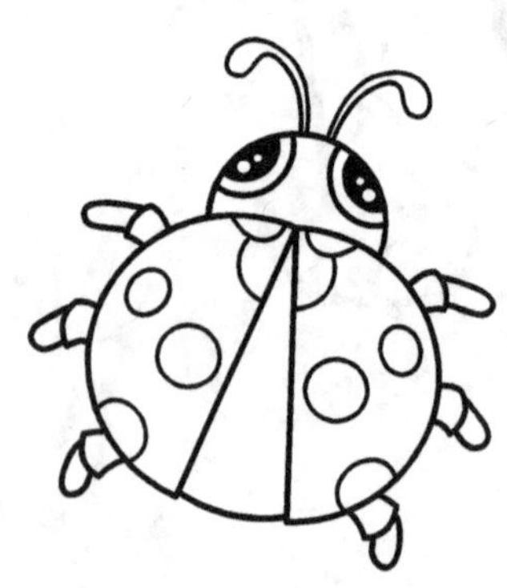

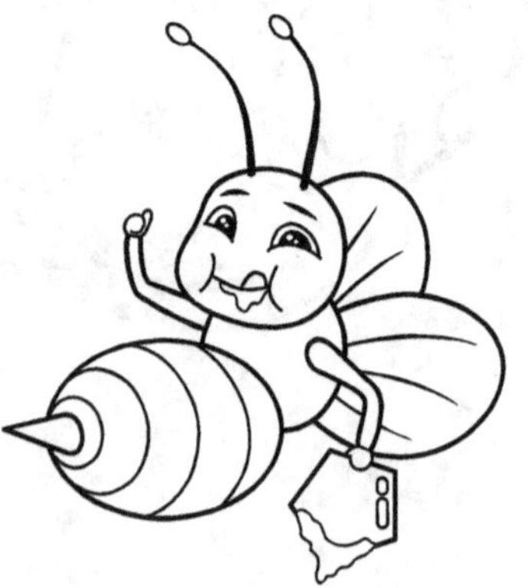

LOVE BIRD

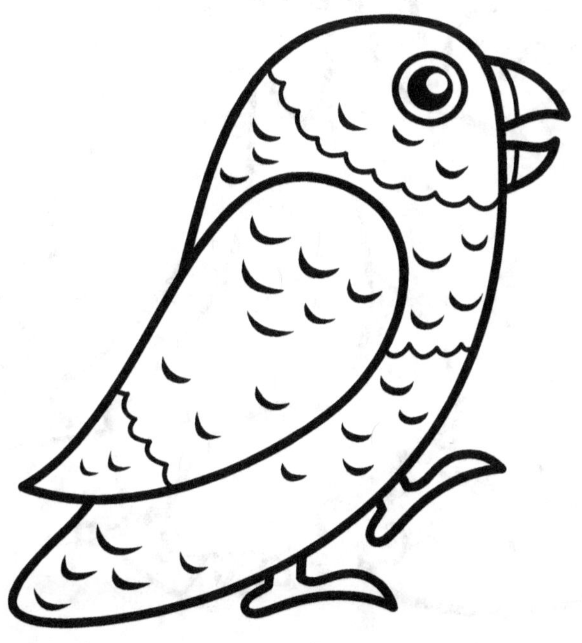

VULTURE

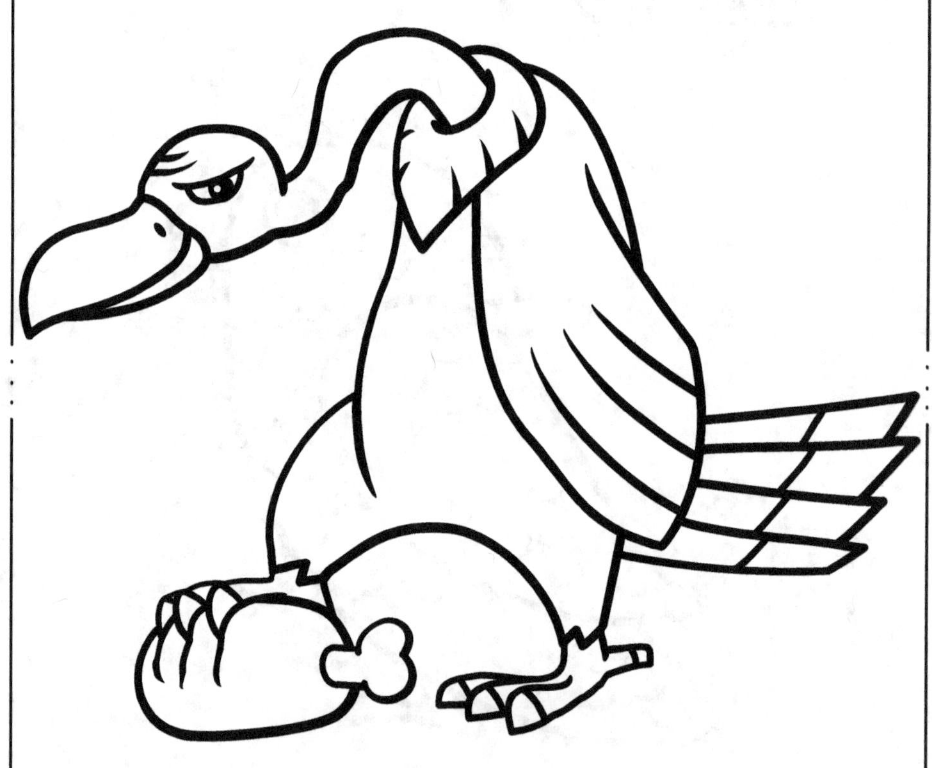

BEE

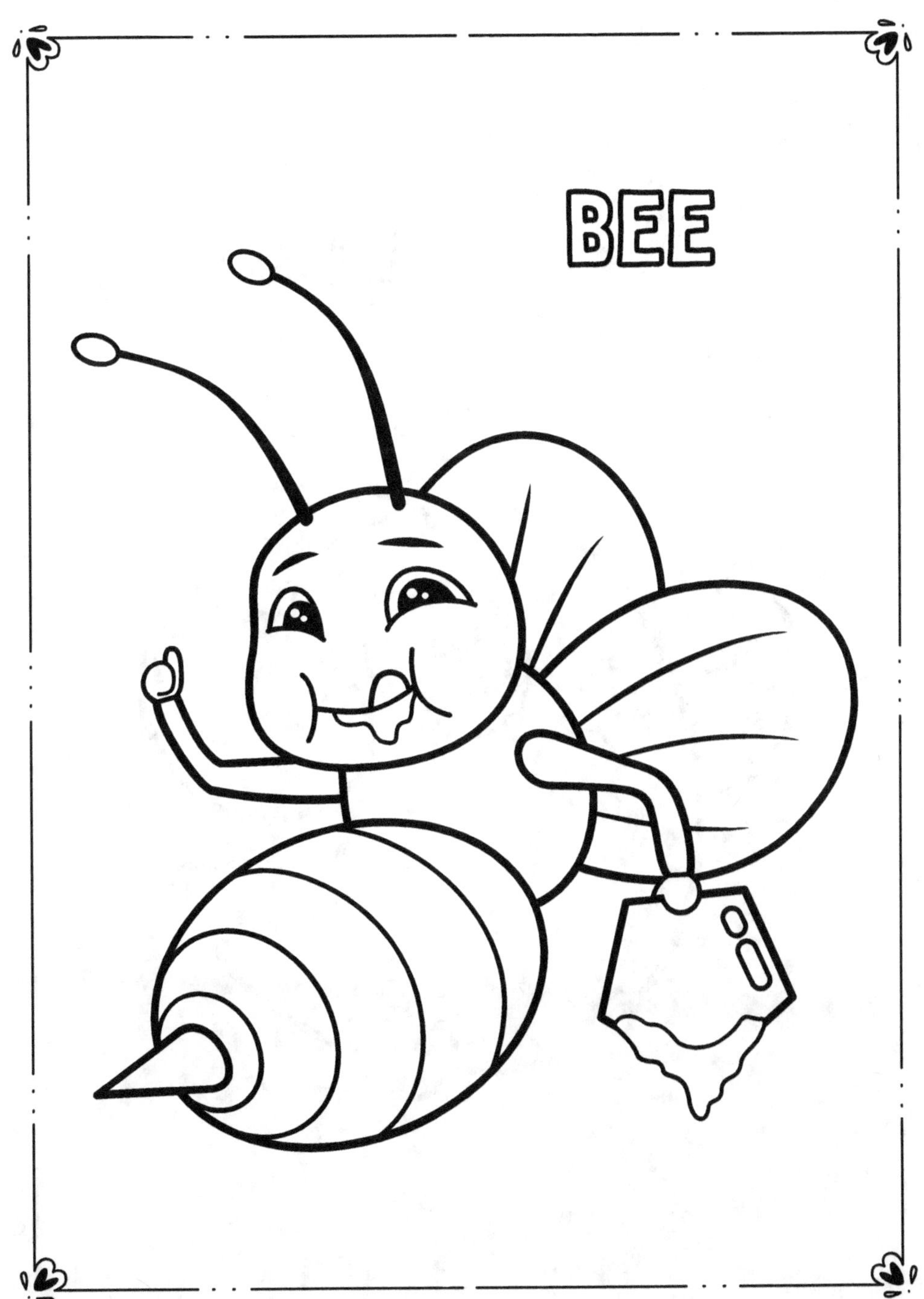

BIRD

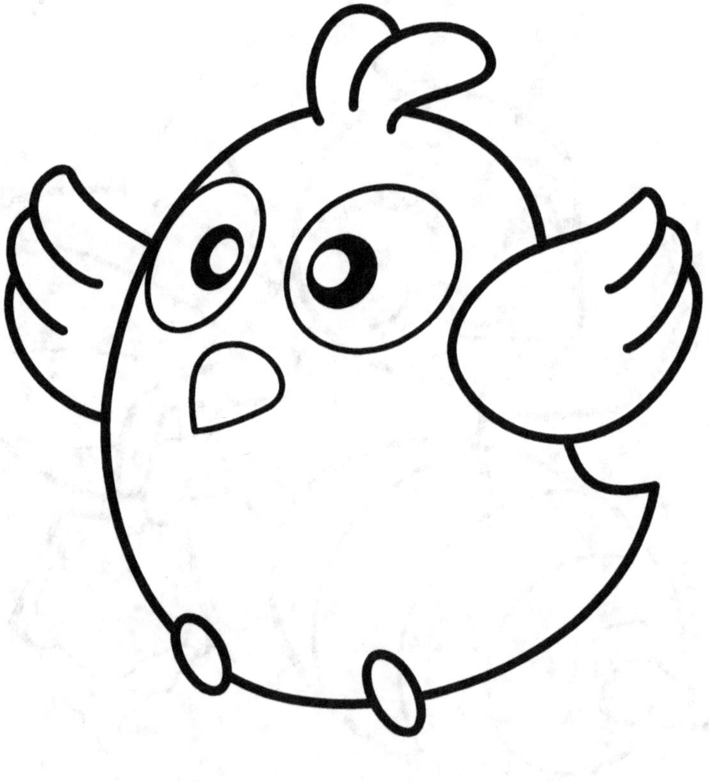

LADYBUG

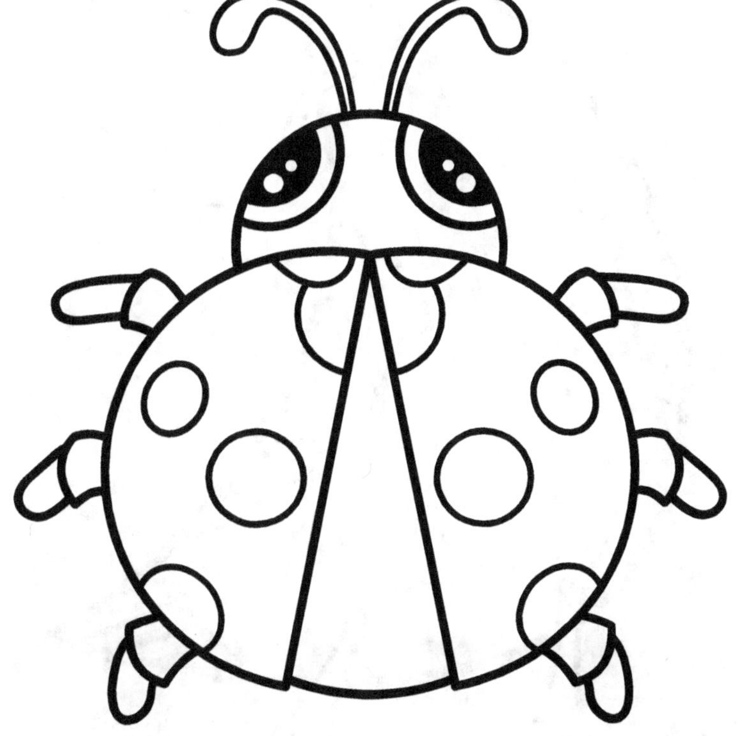

INCA TERN

SEAGULL

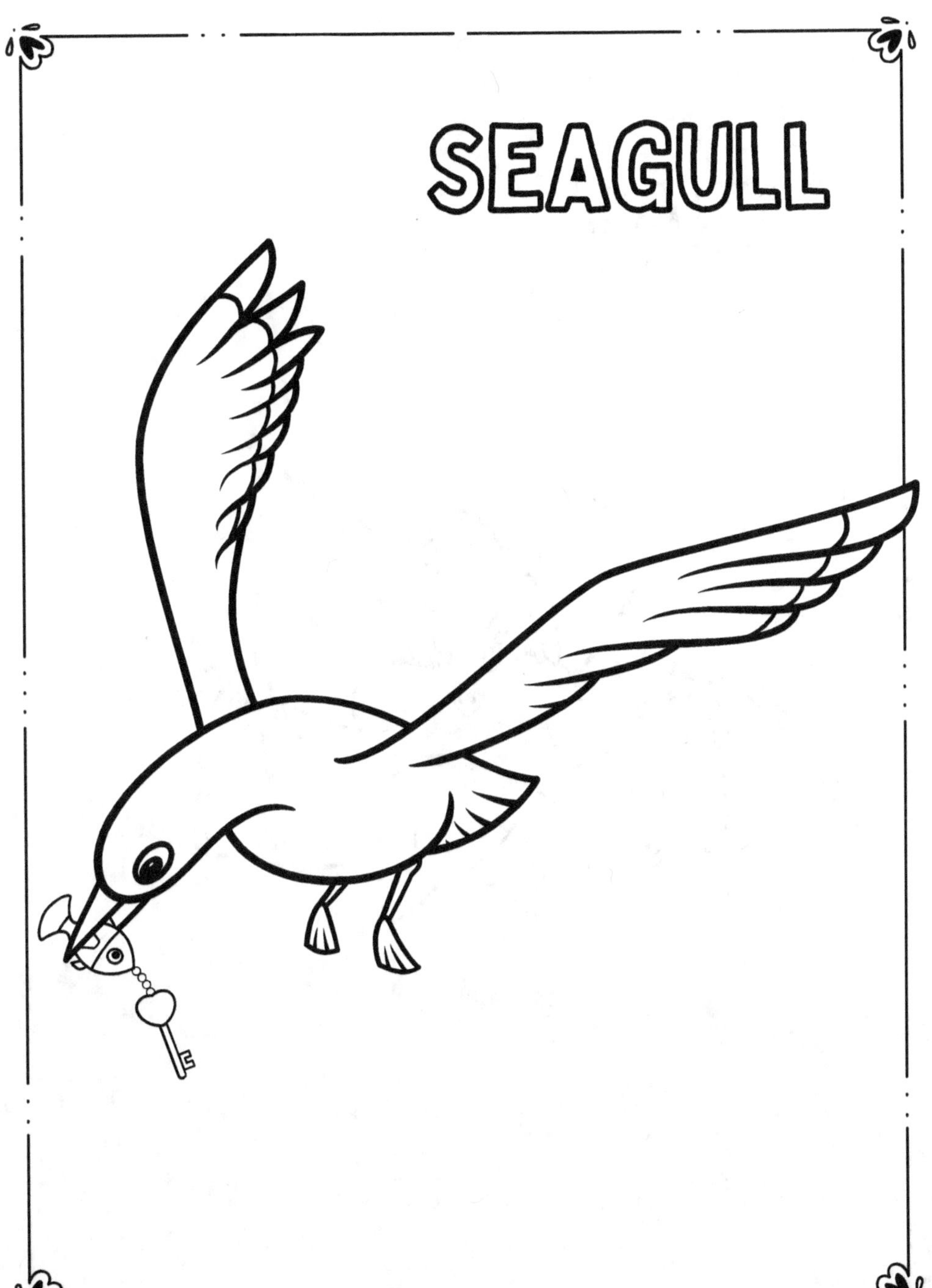

BAT

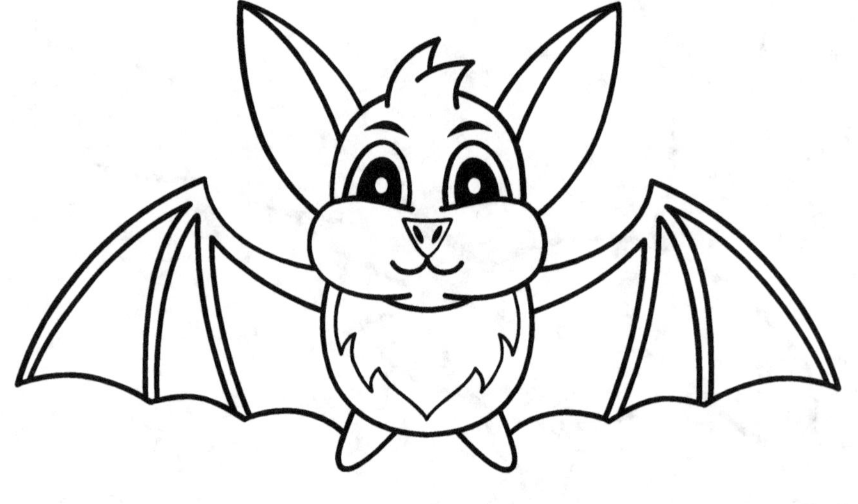

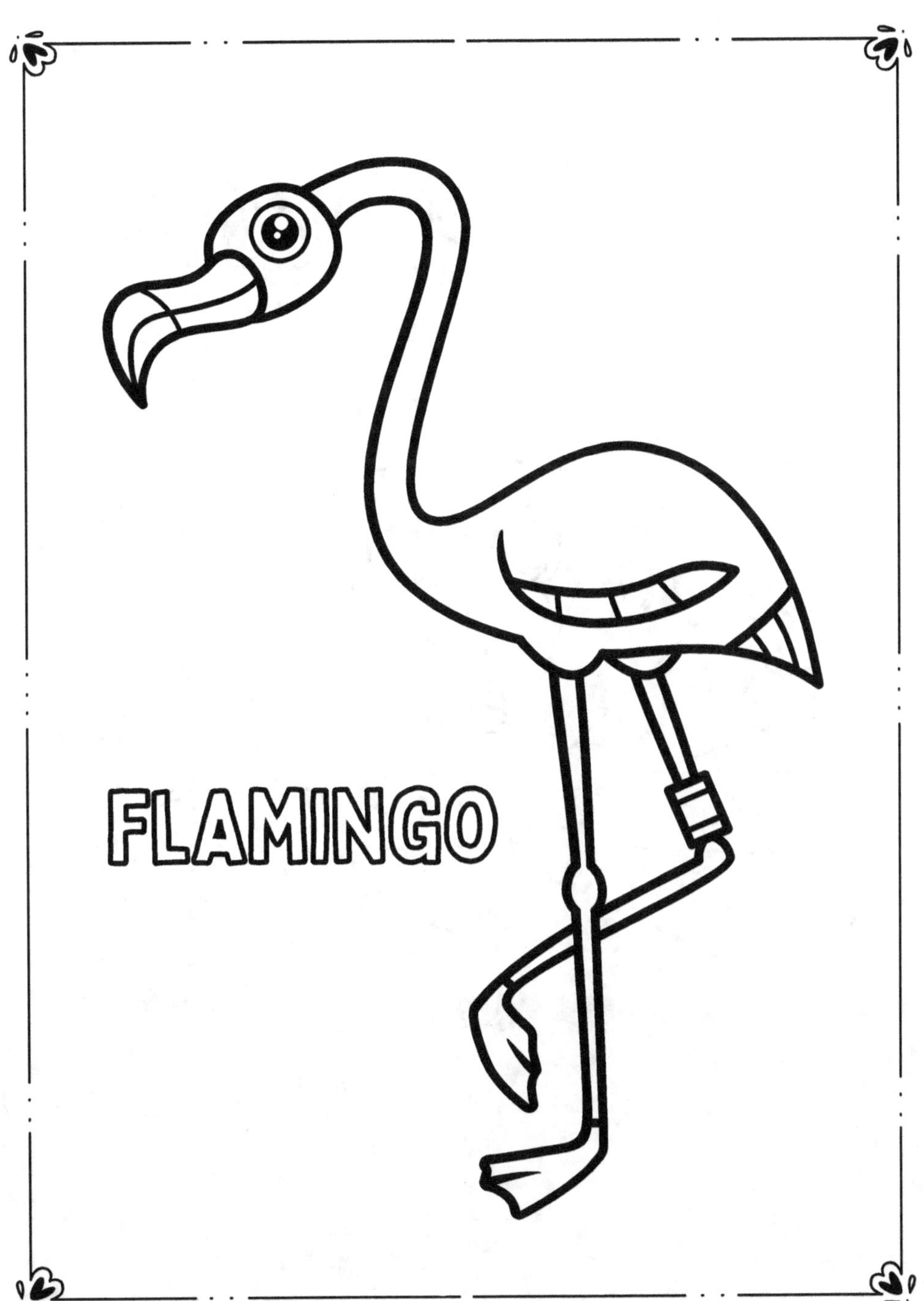

FLAMINGO

PEACOCK

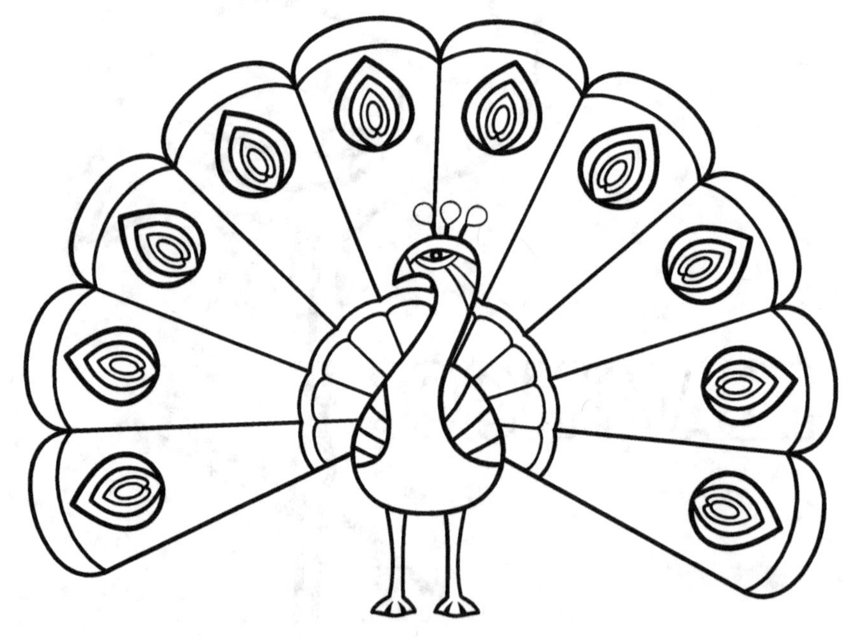

SPARROW

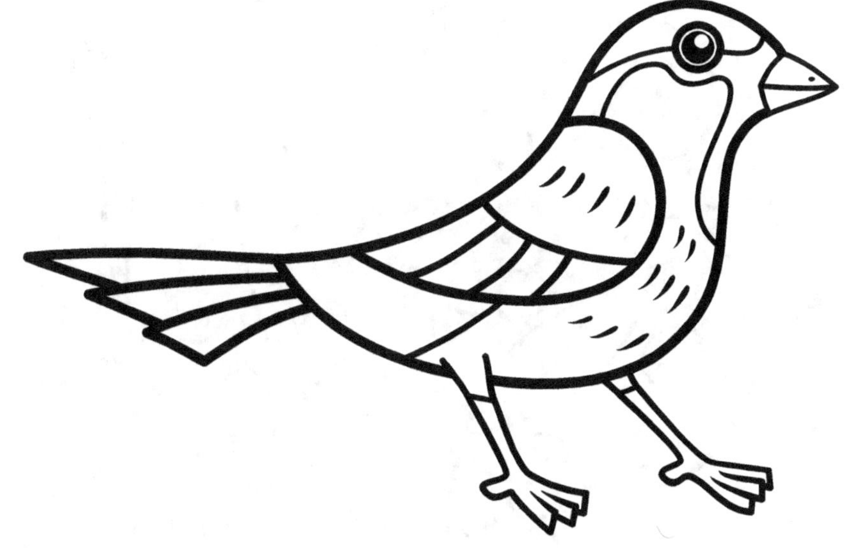

BUTTERFLY

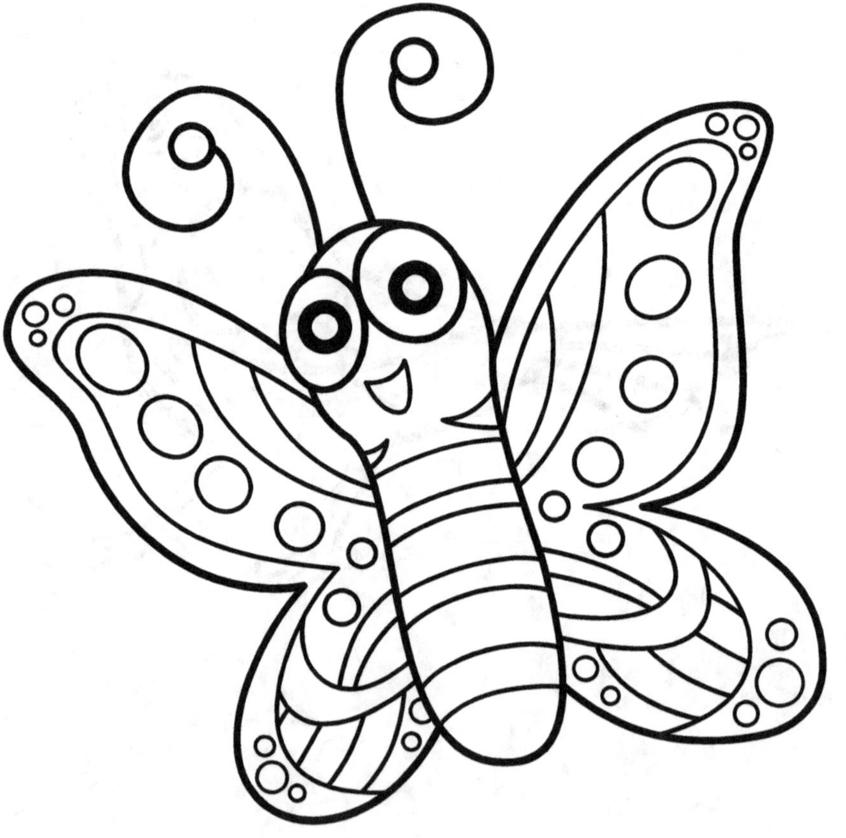

MOTH

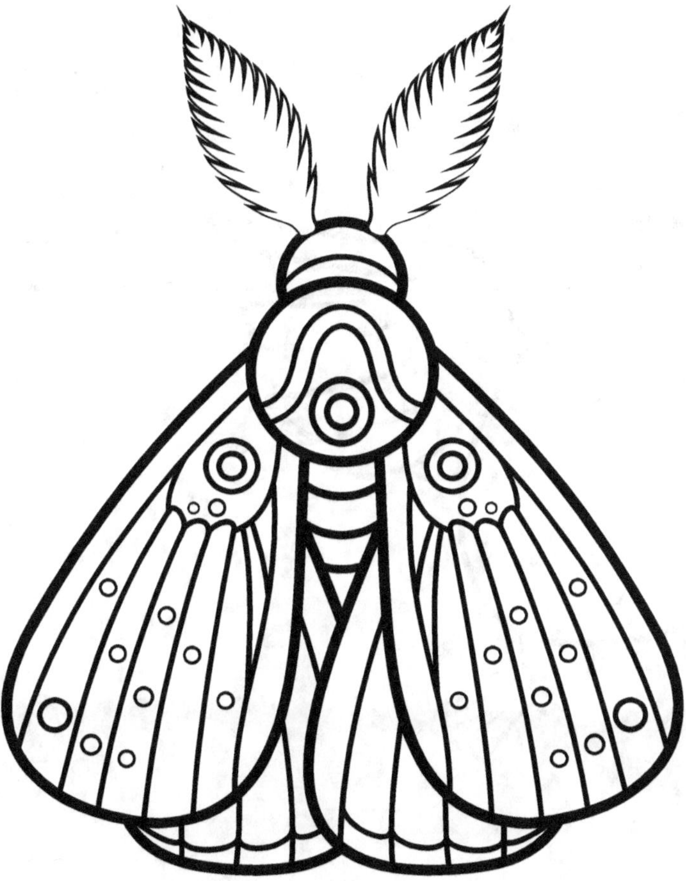

PIGEON

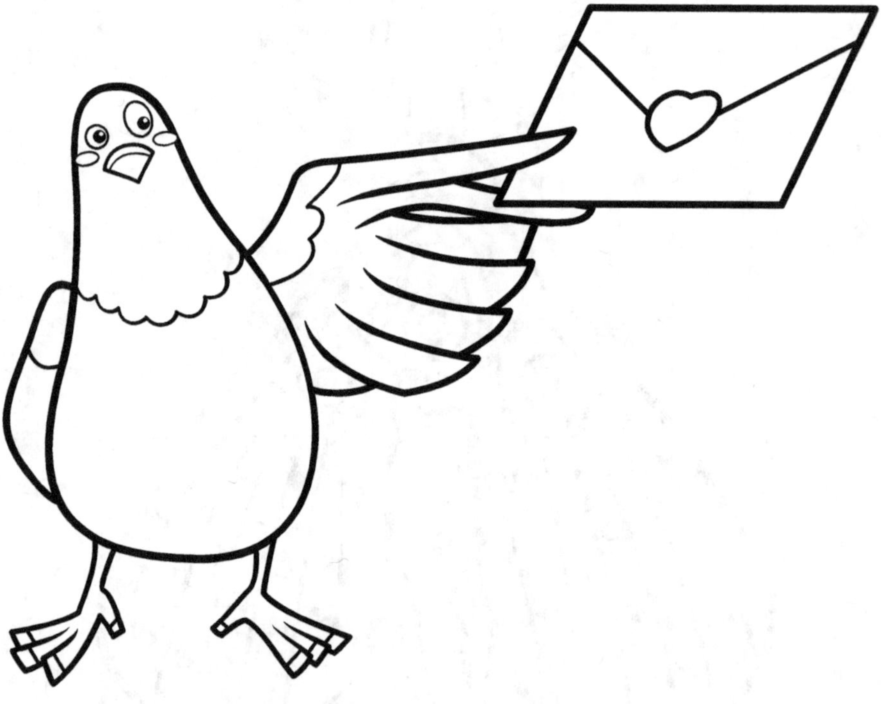

OWL

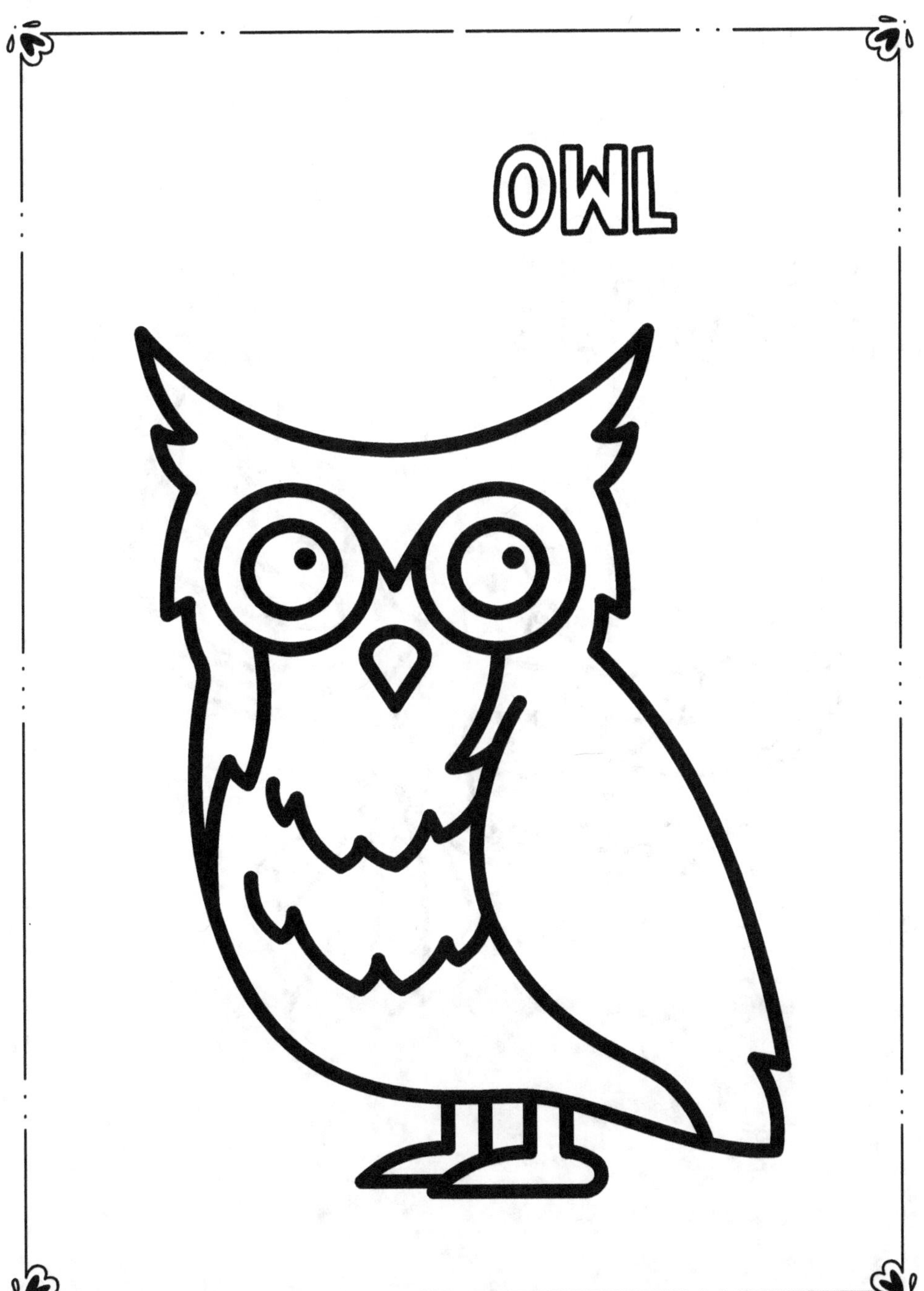

MAGPIE

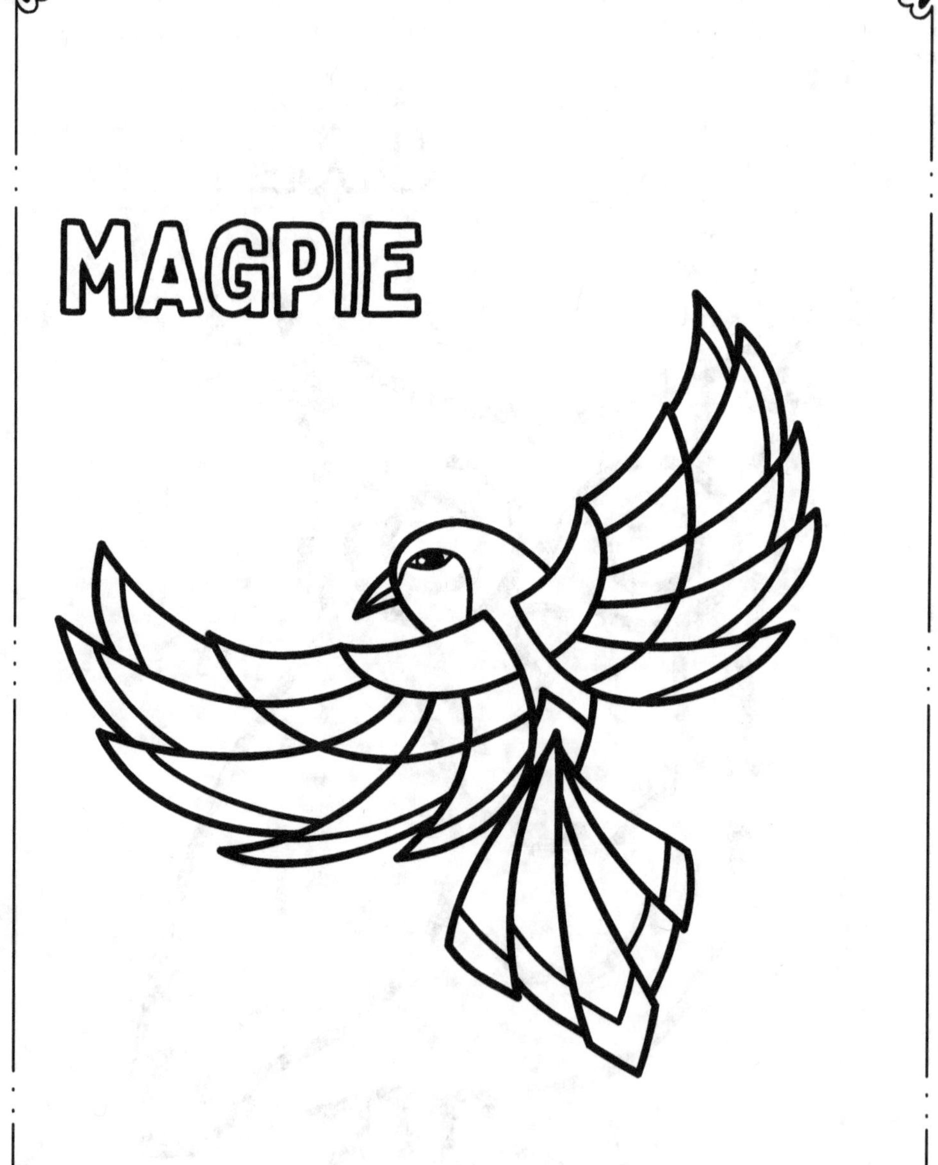

PELICAN

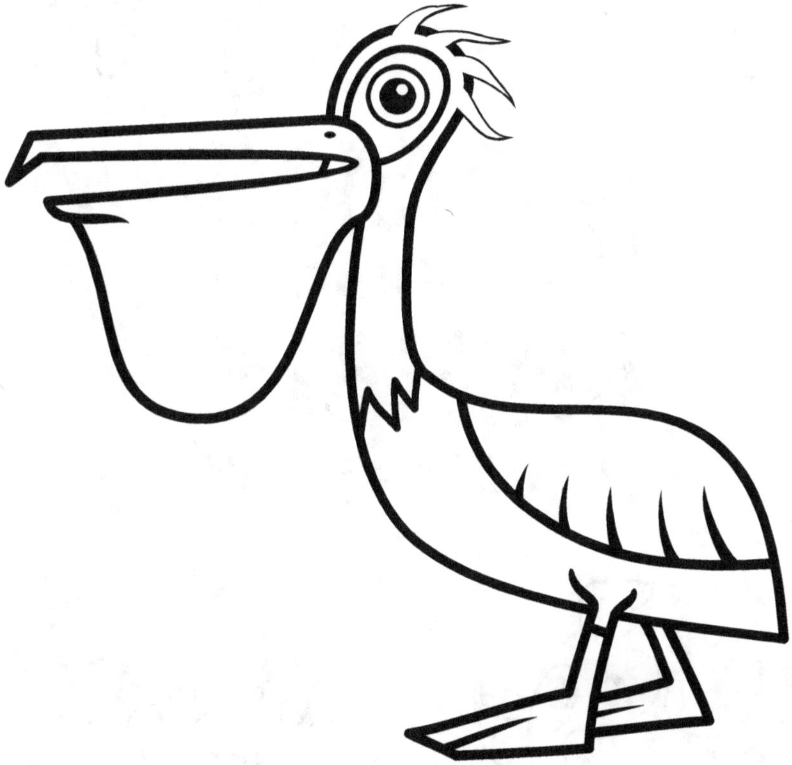

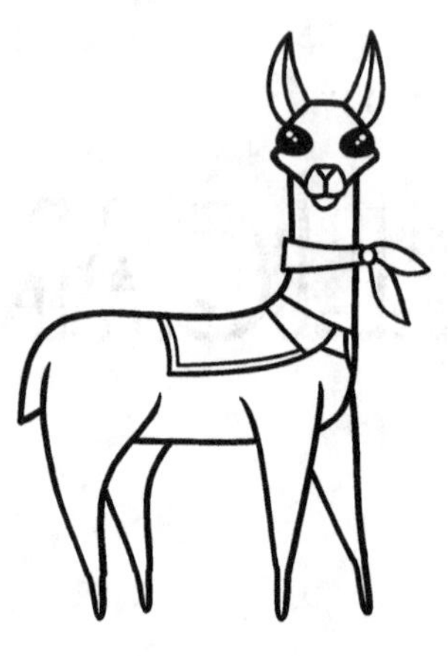 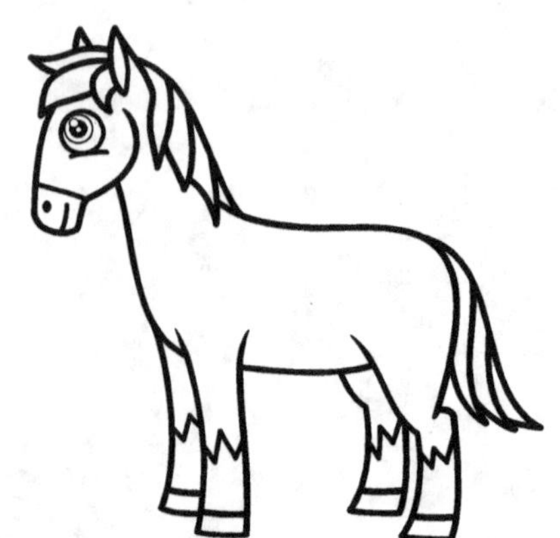

FARM
ANIMALS
COLORING BOOK

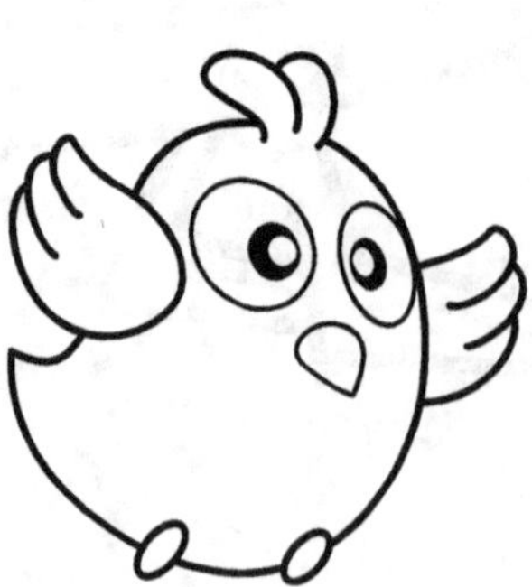 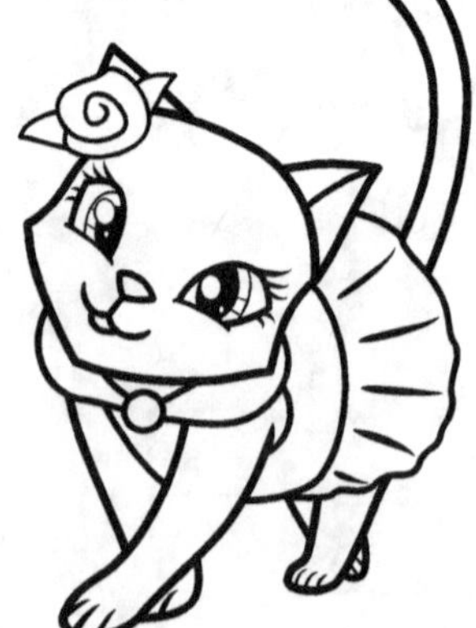

CAT

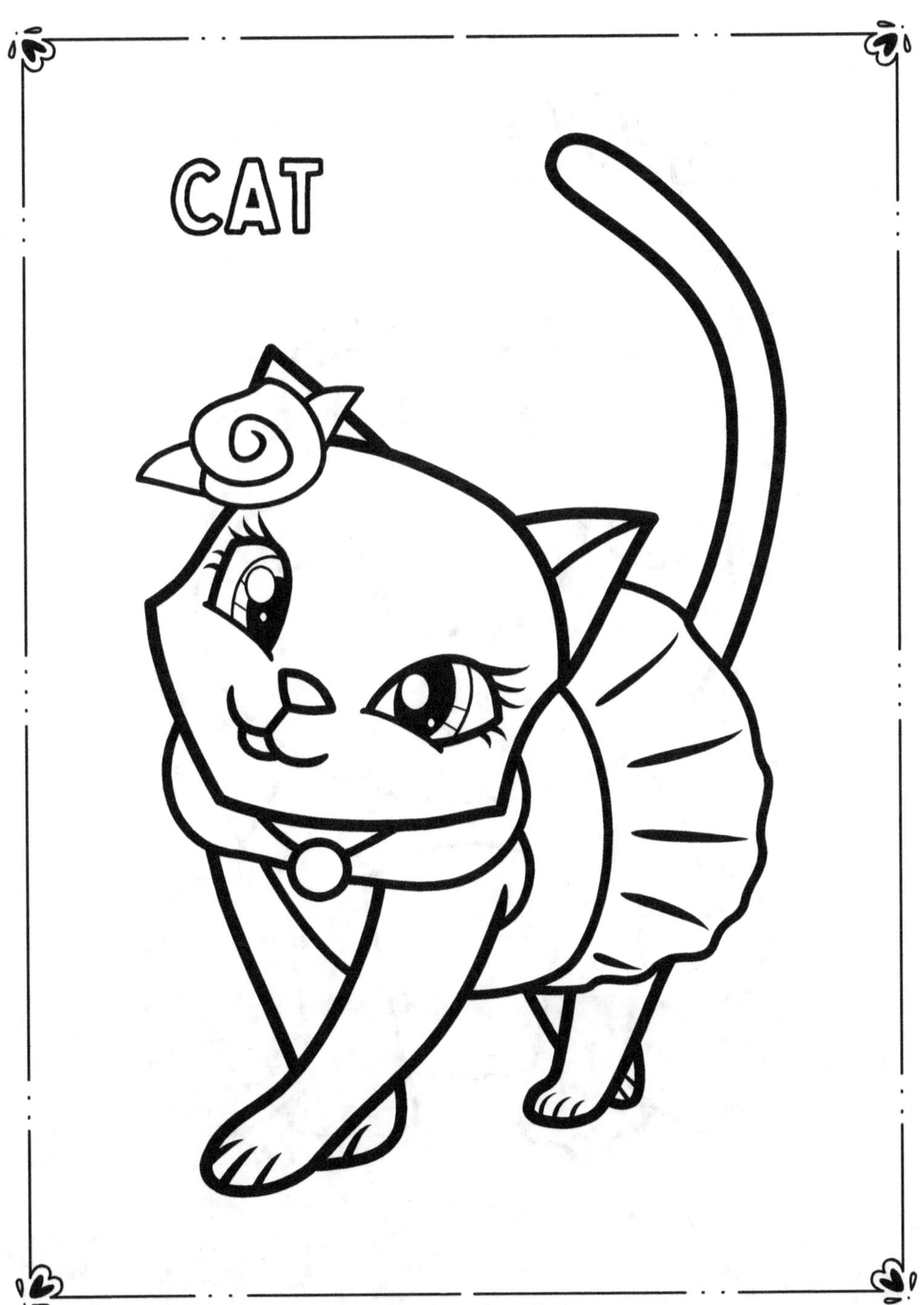

FROG

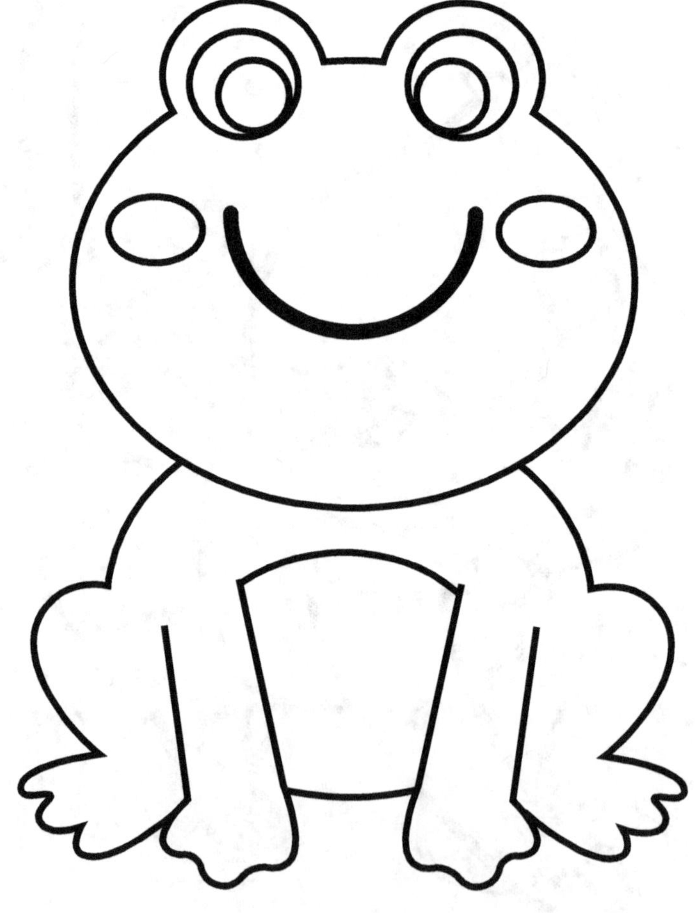

COW

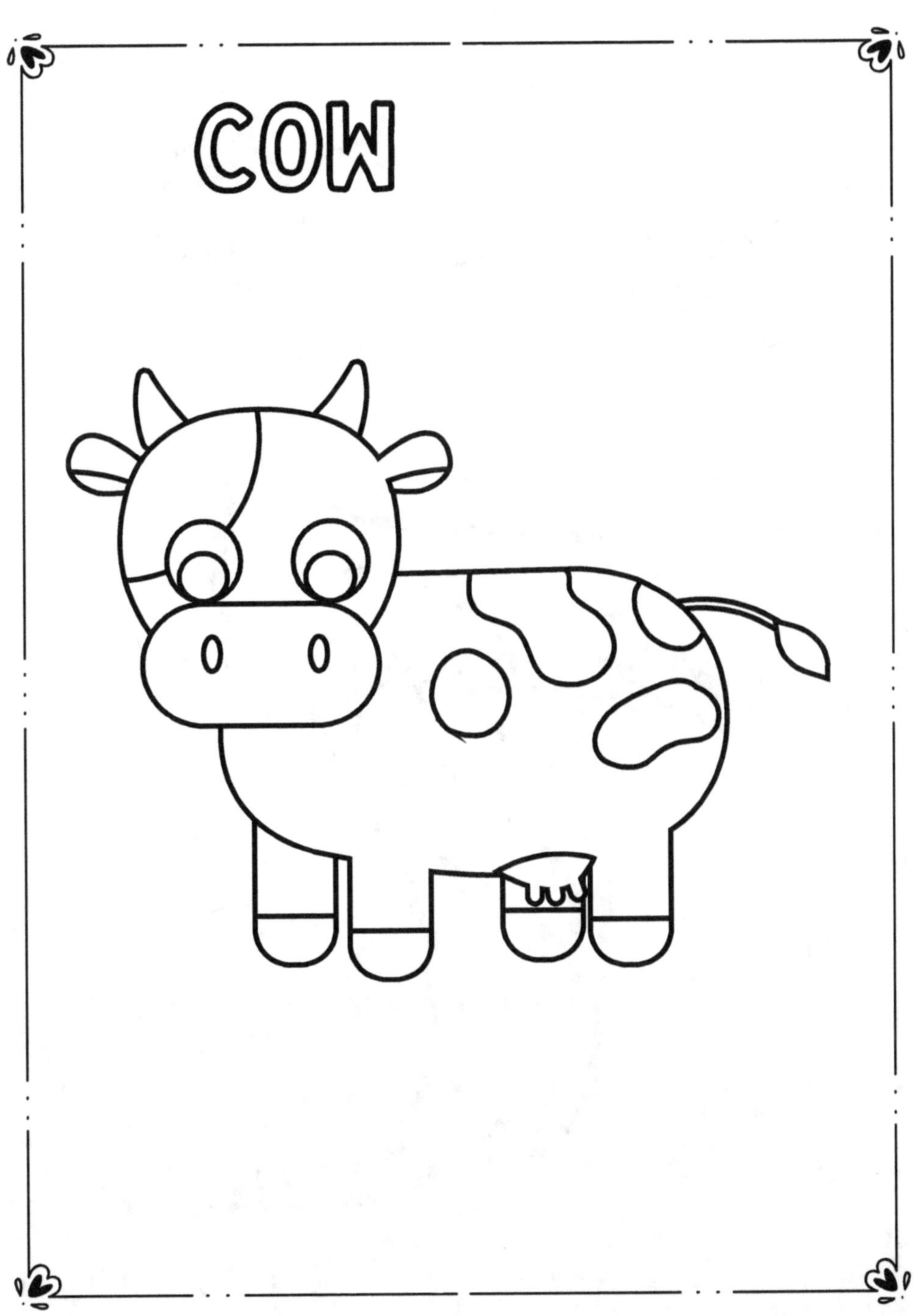

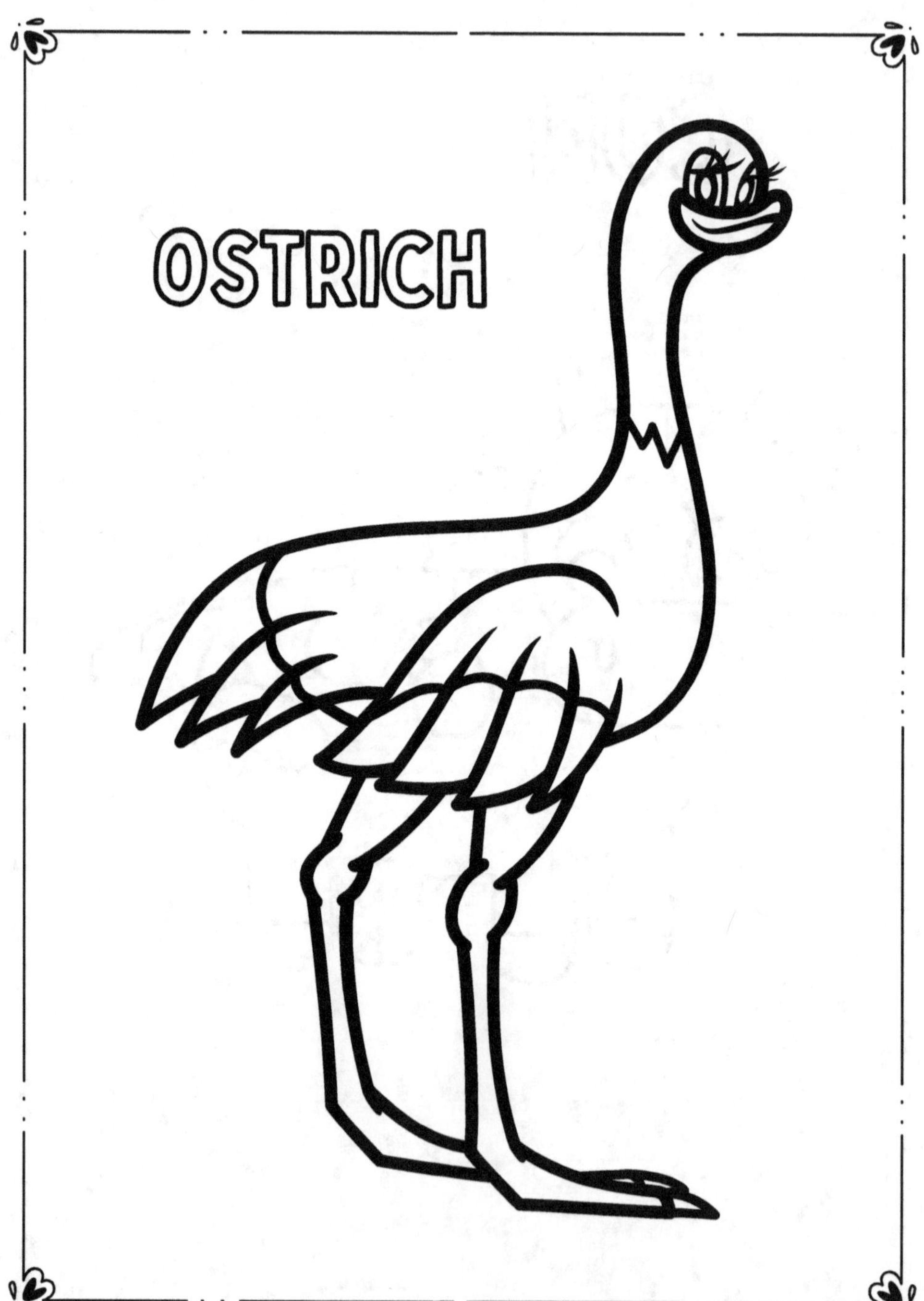

OSTRICH

BULL

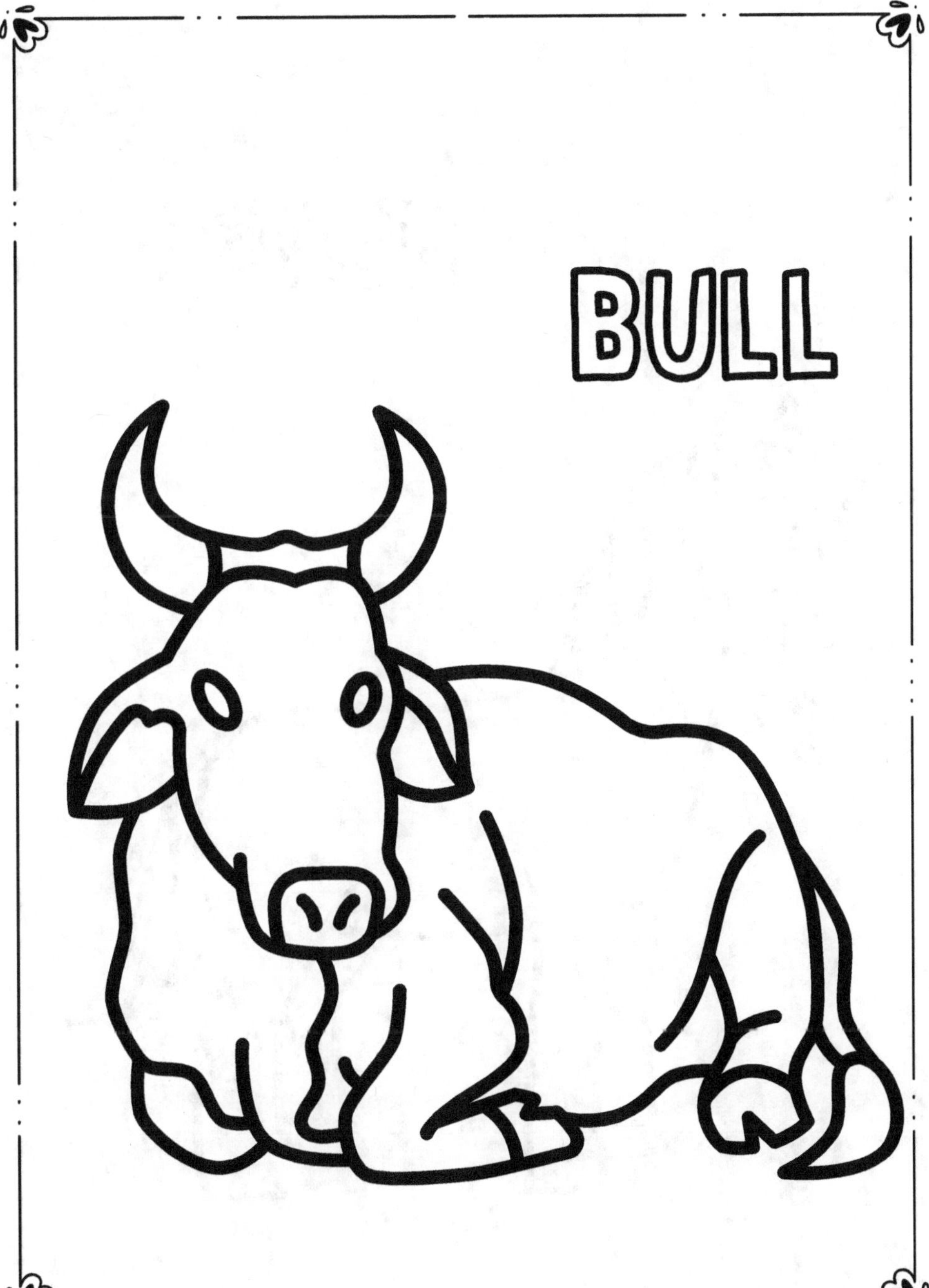

HORSE

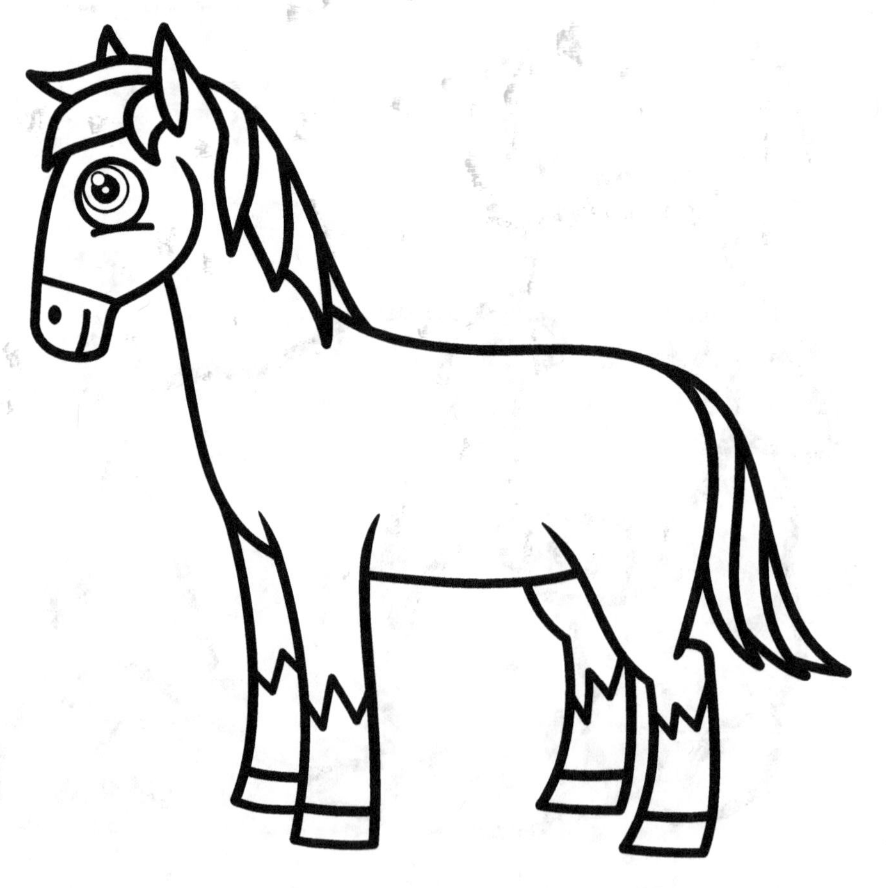

DUCK

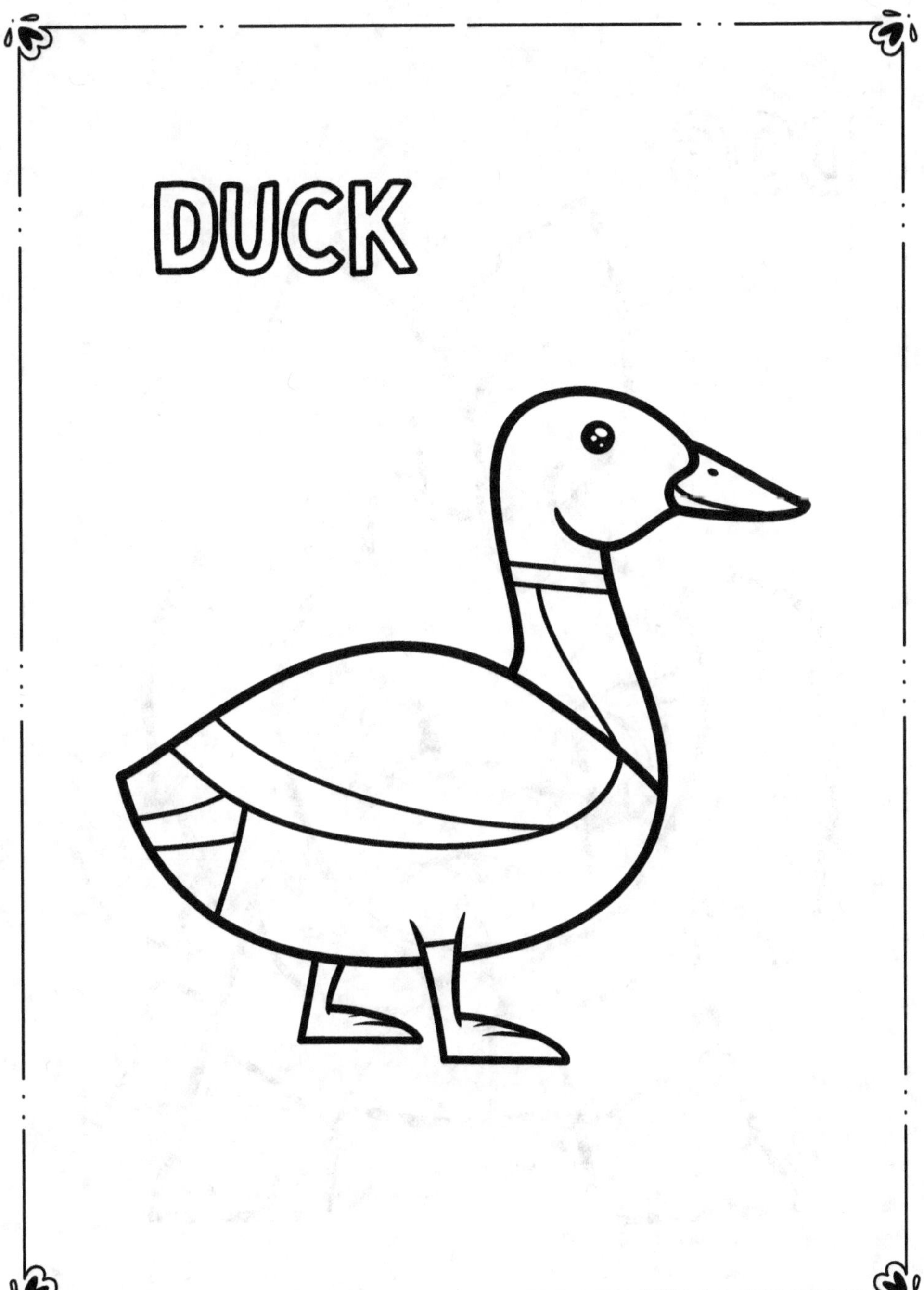

DOG

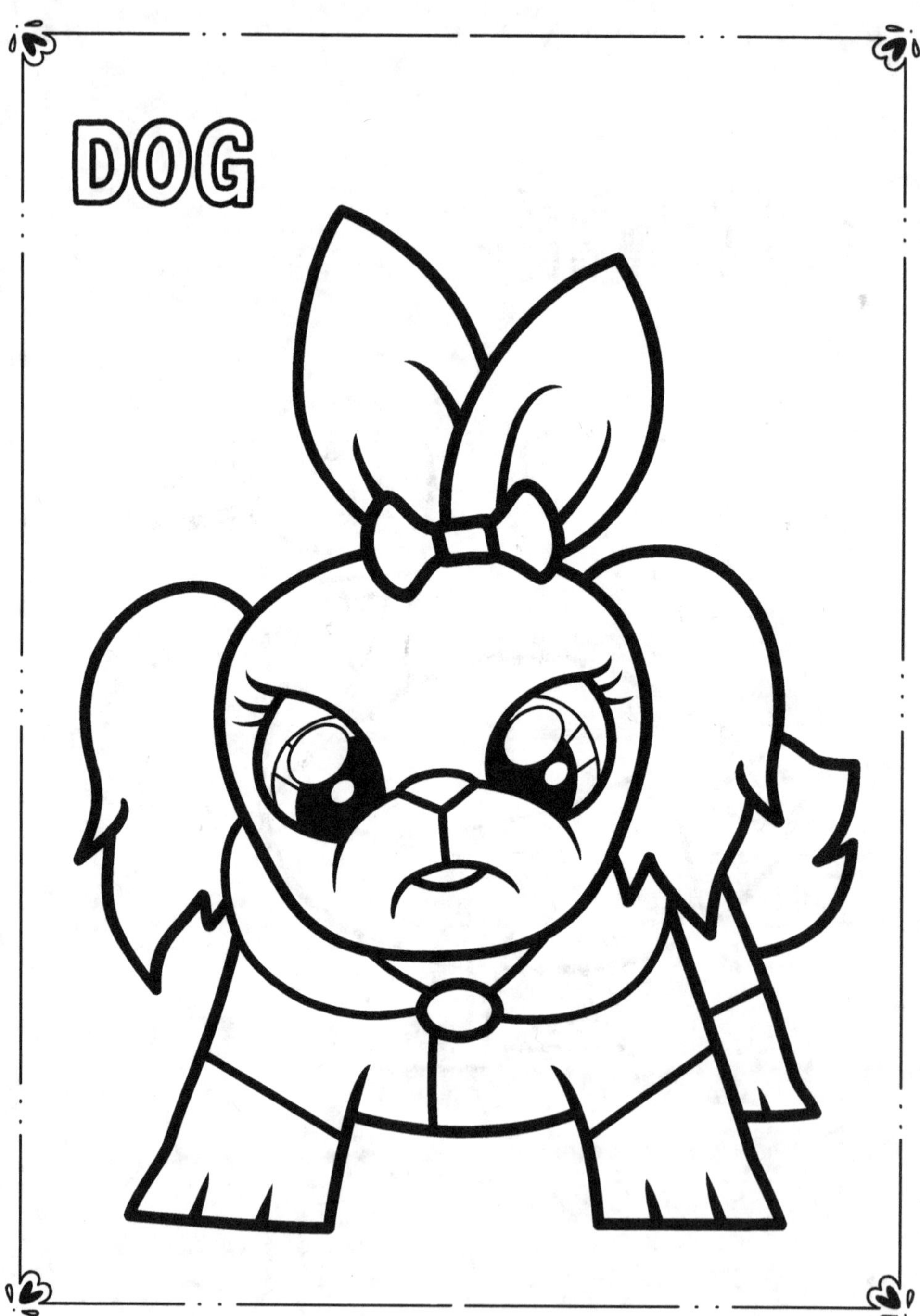

GEESE

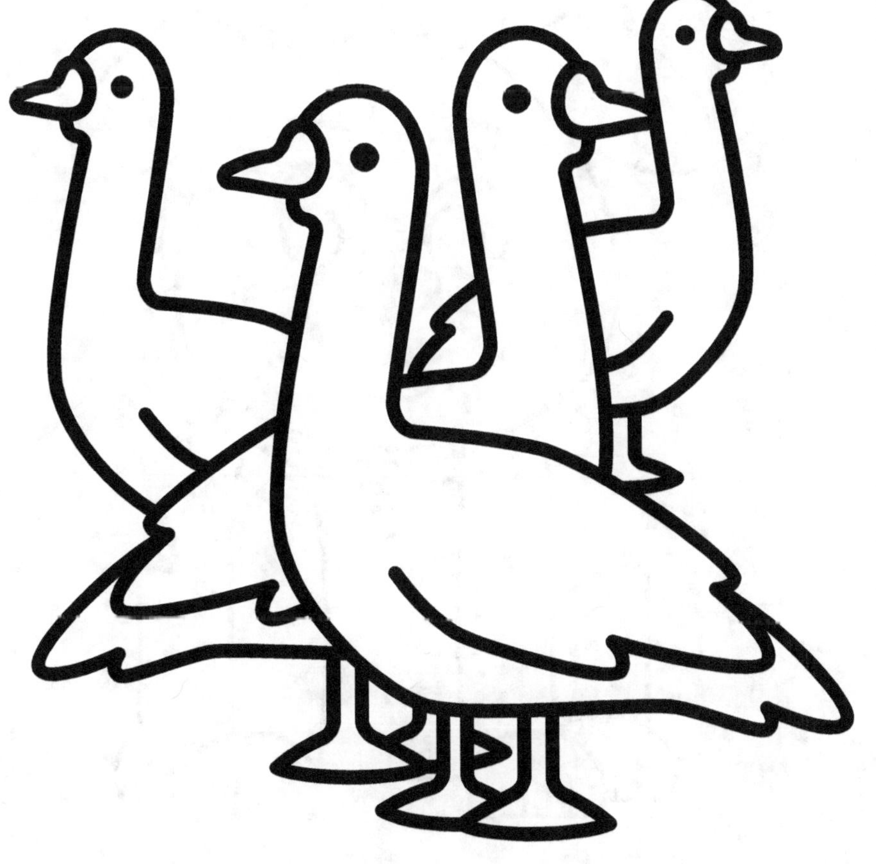

DOG

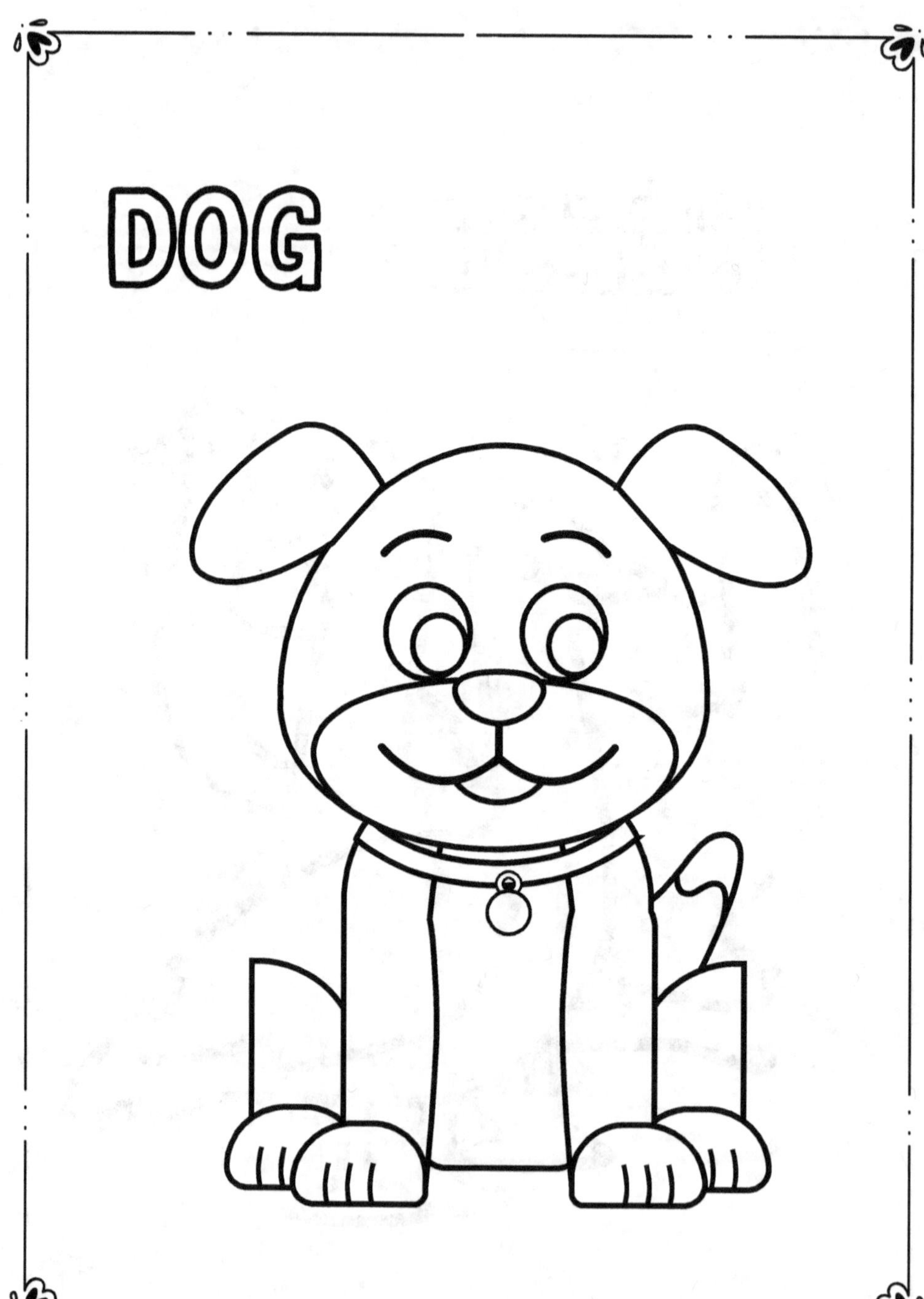

PIG

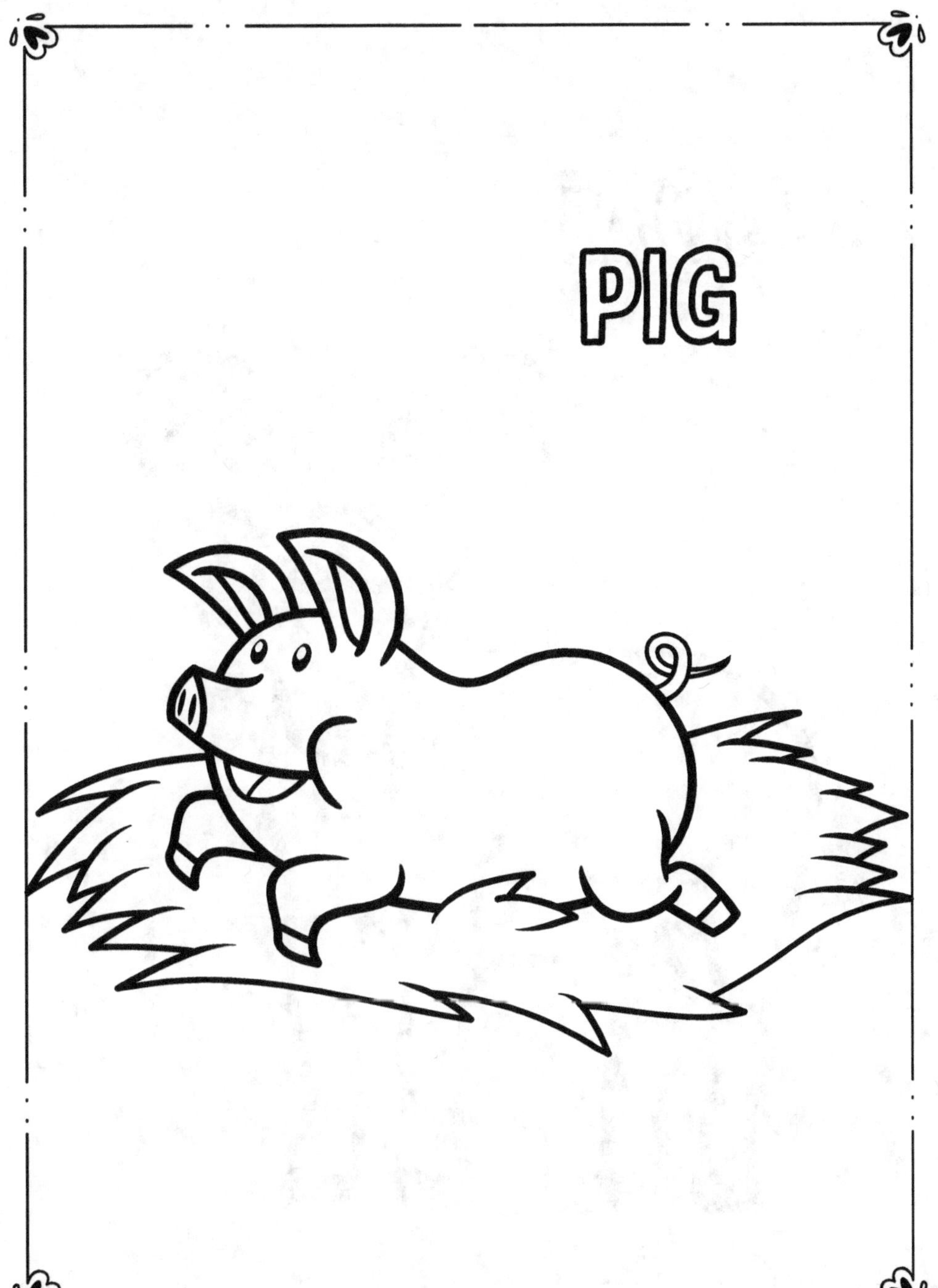

GOAT

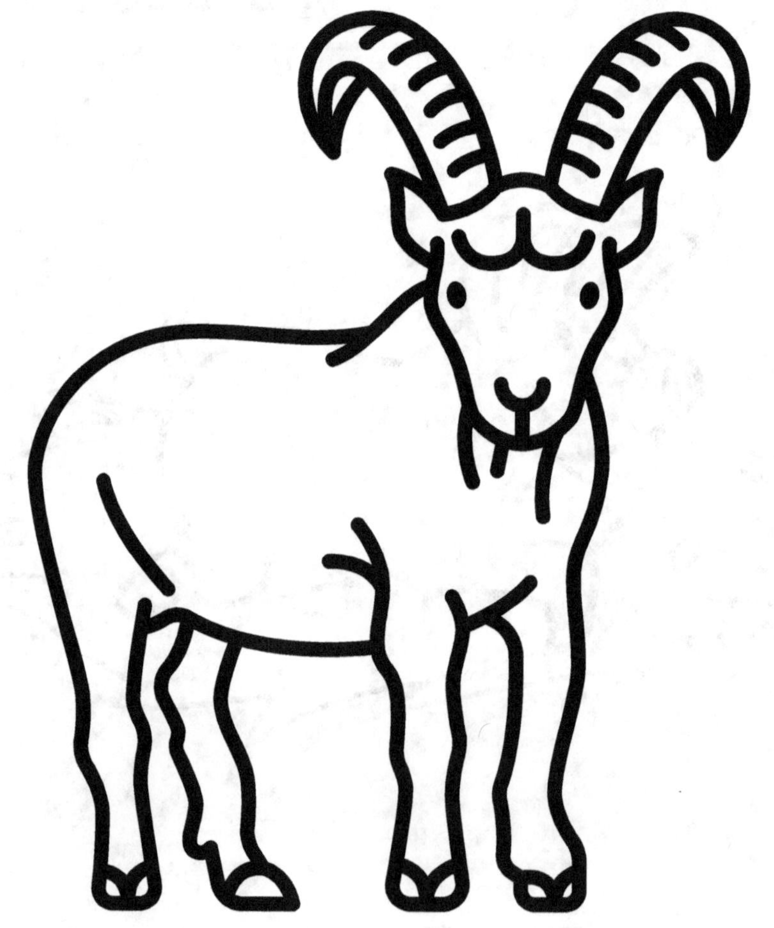

OTTER

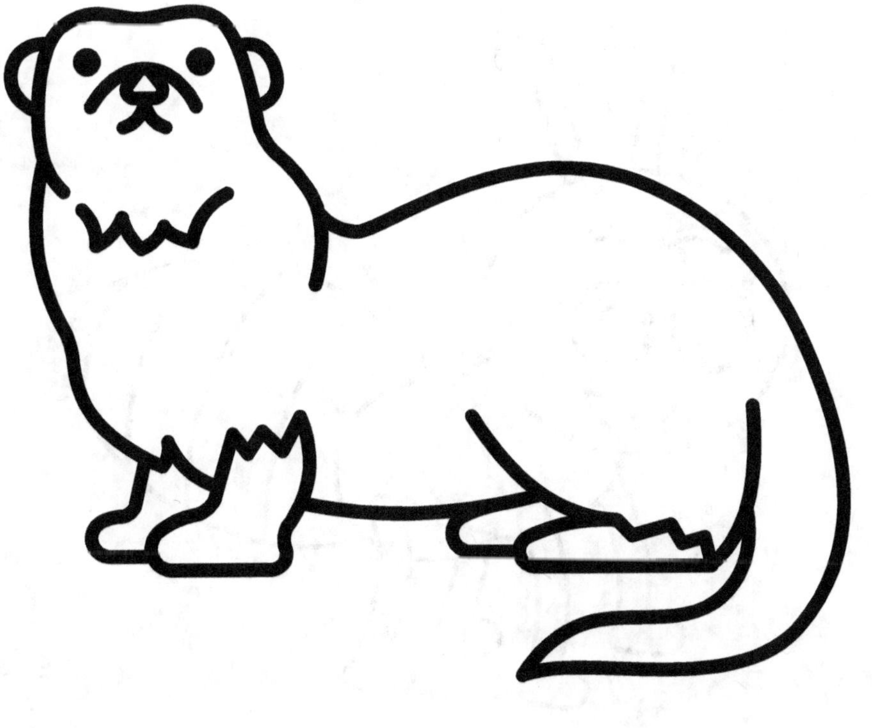

ANT

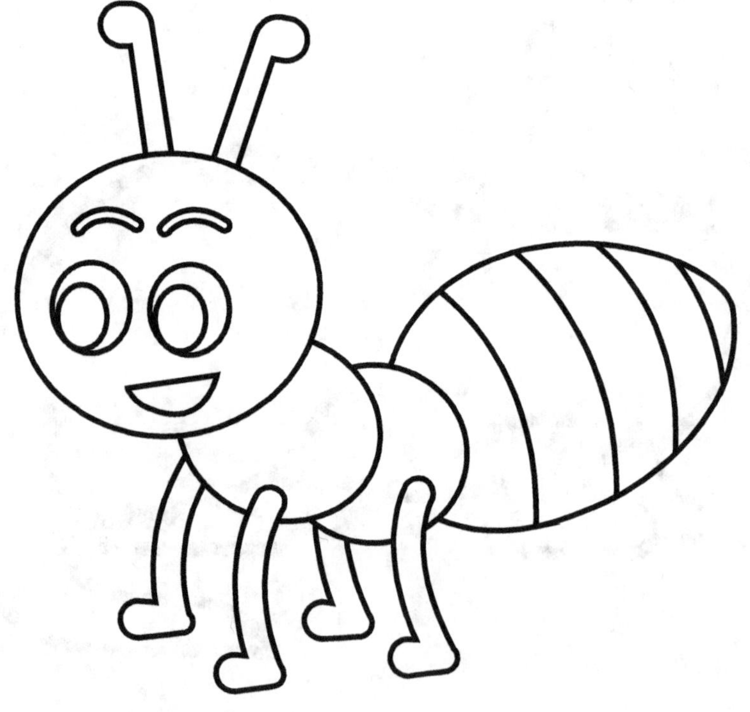

DONKEY

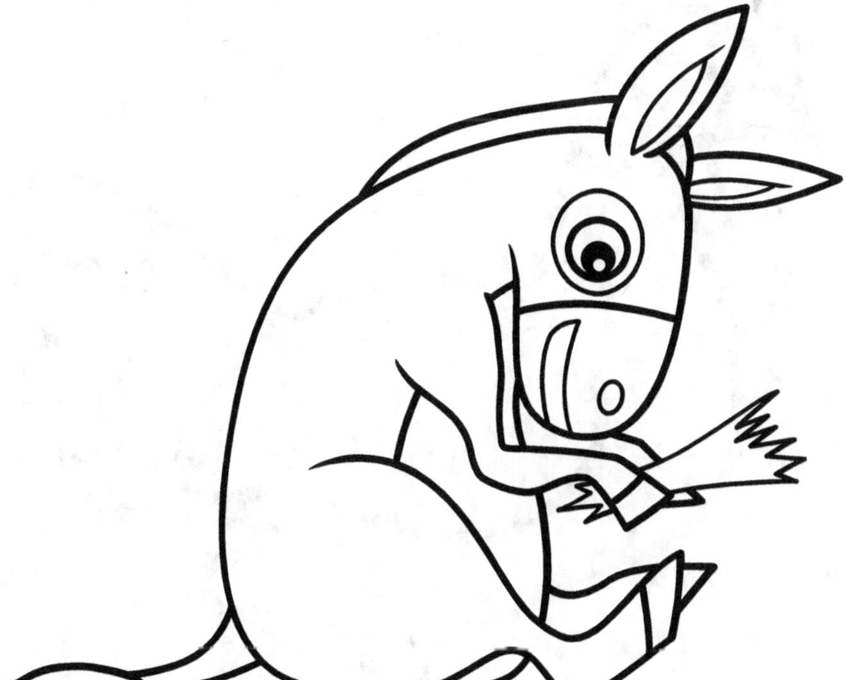

CHICKEN

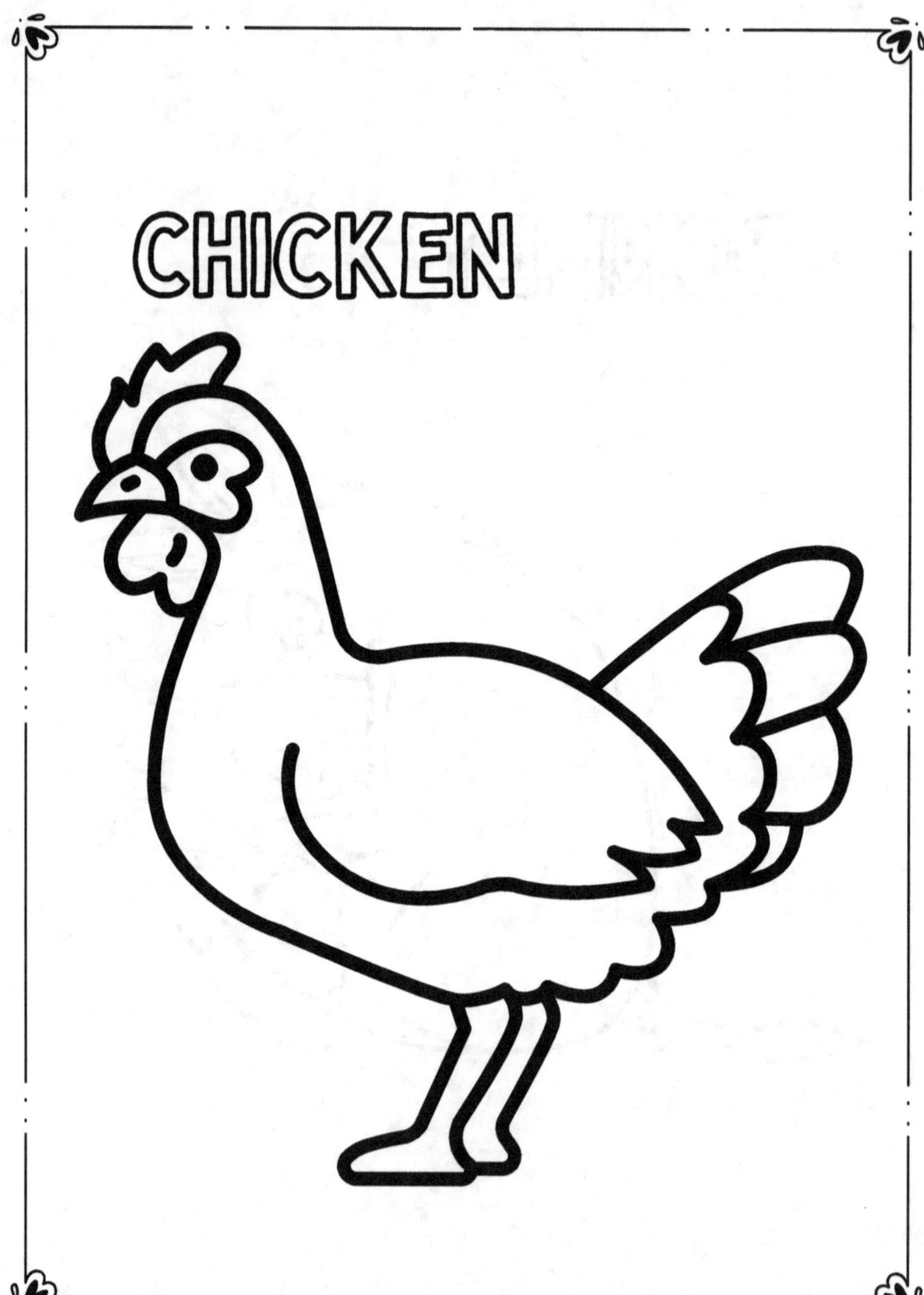

MOUSE

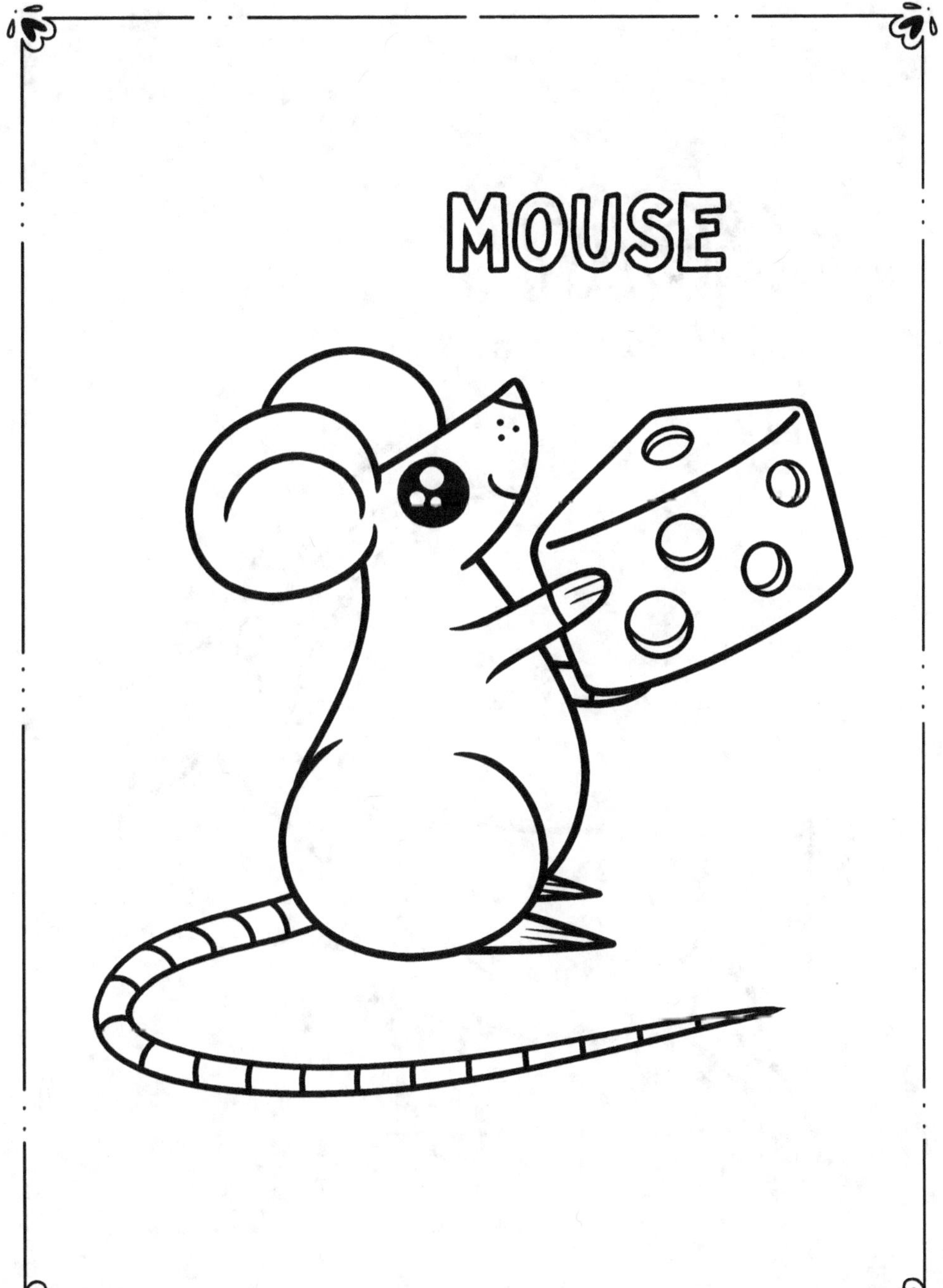

GOAT

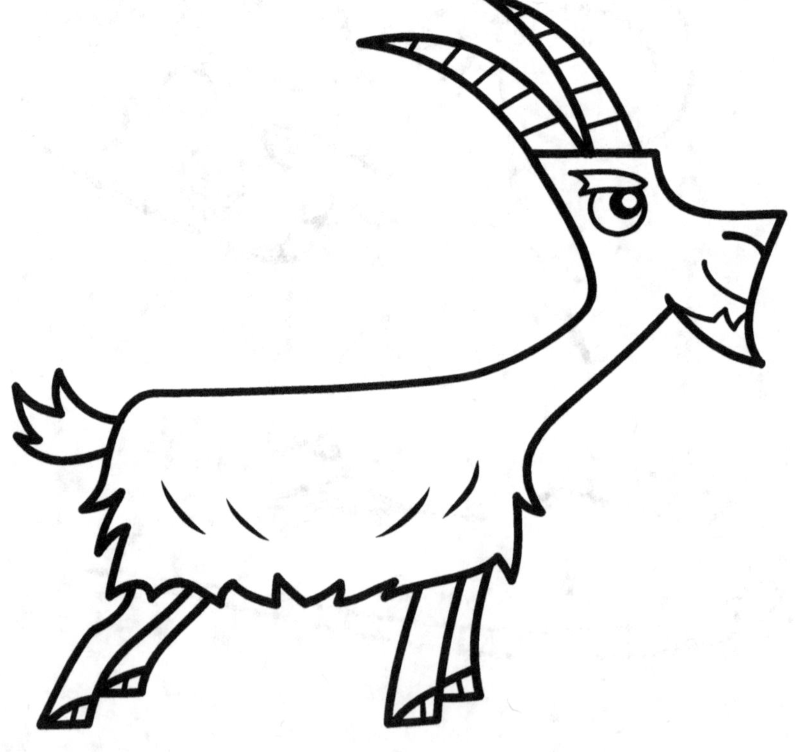

SHEEP

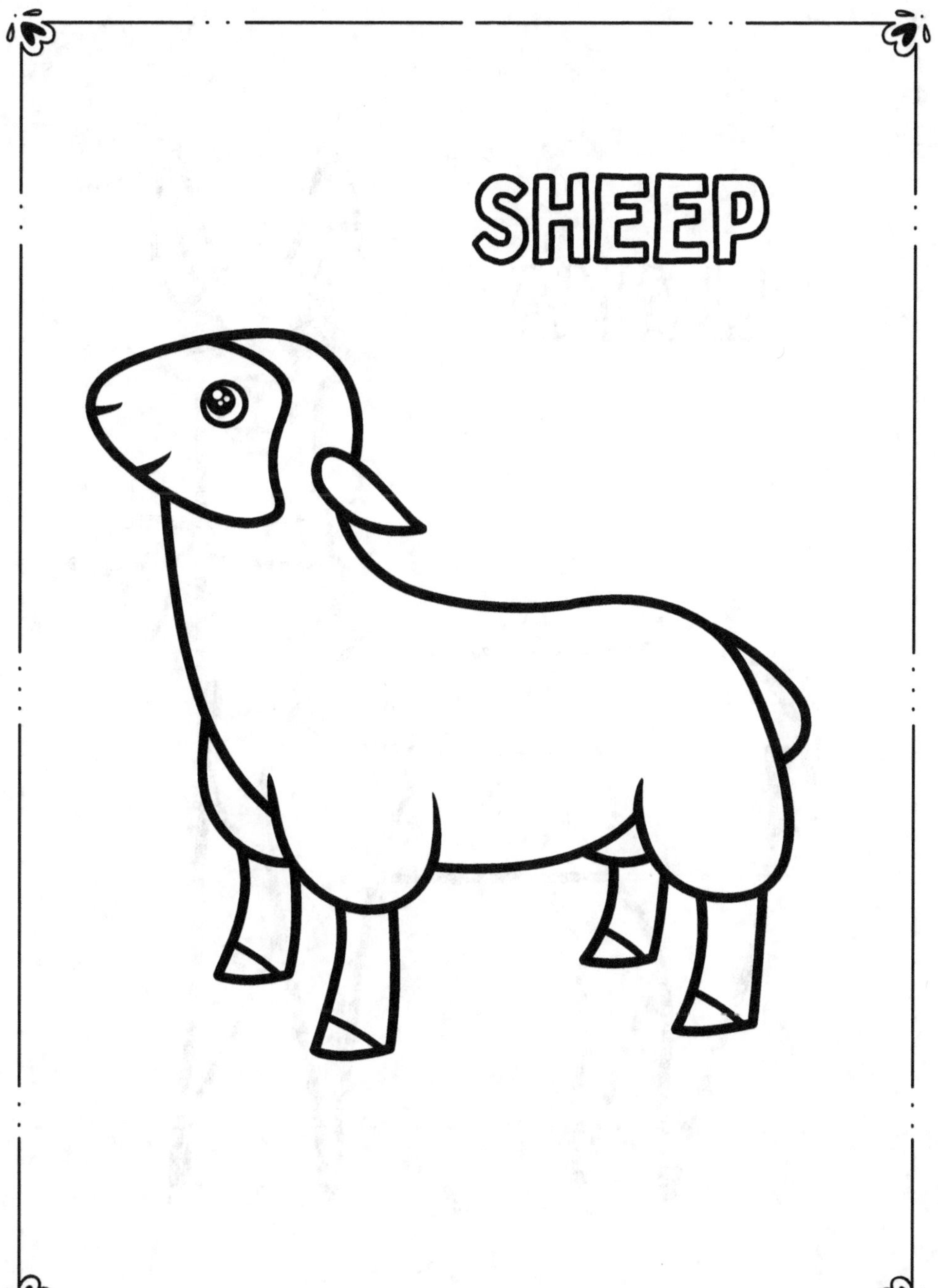

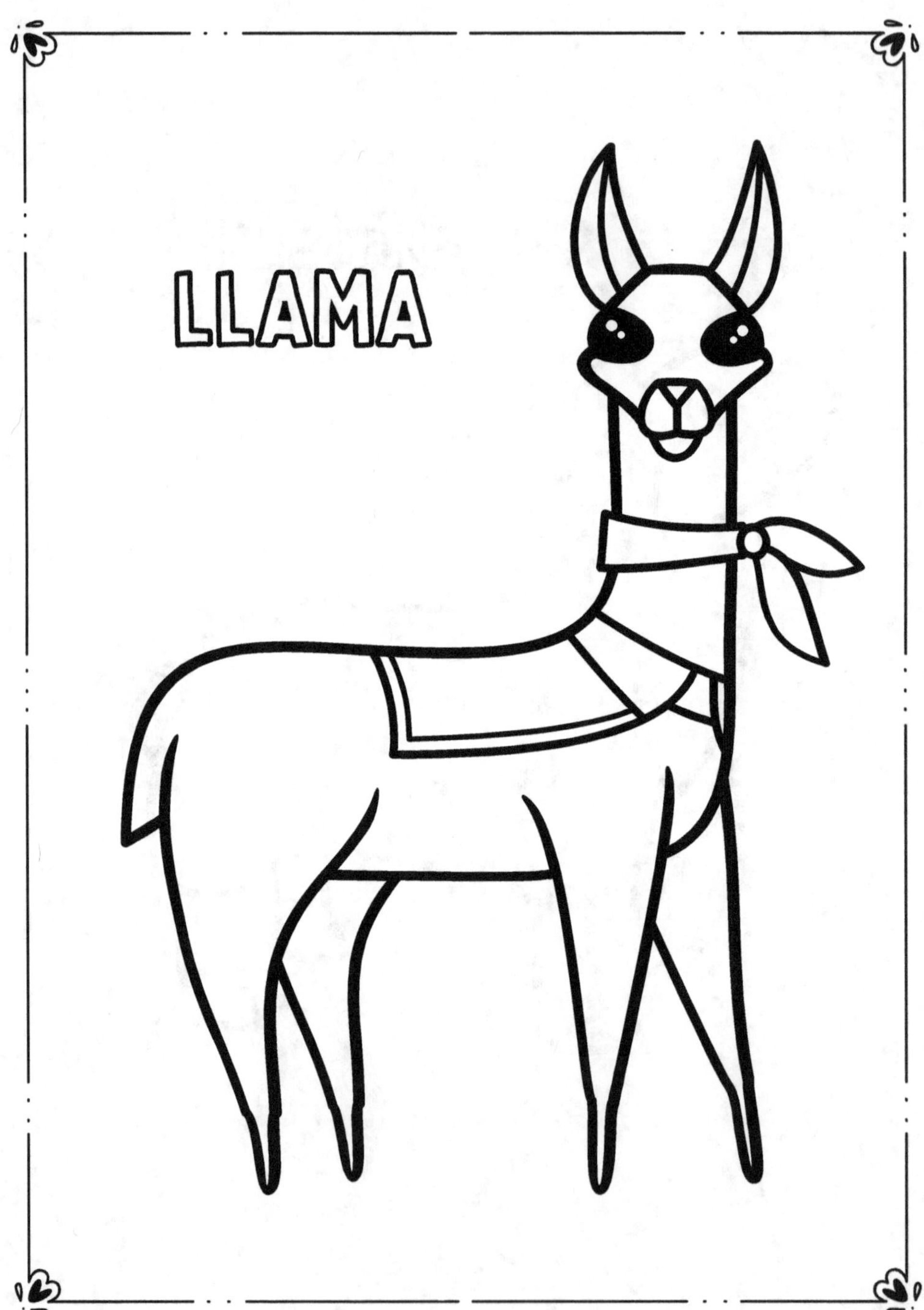

LLAMA

TOAD

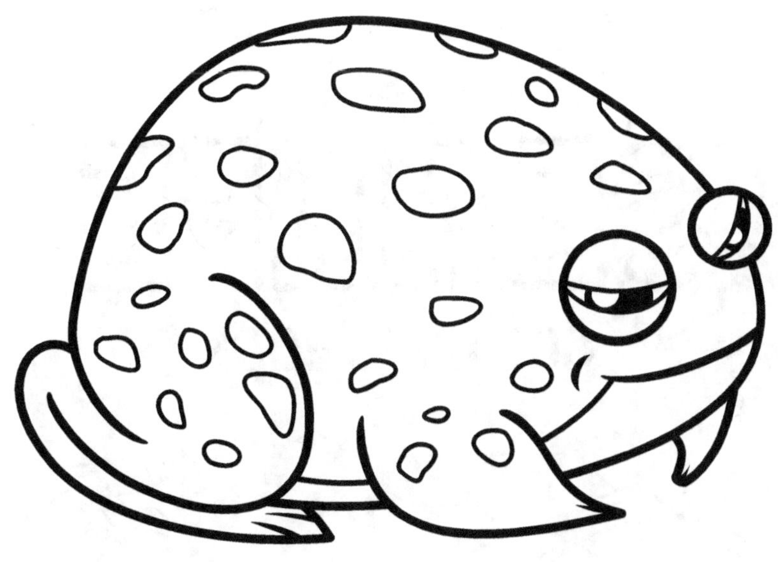

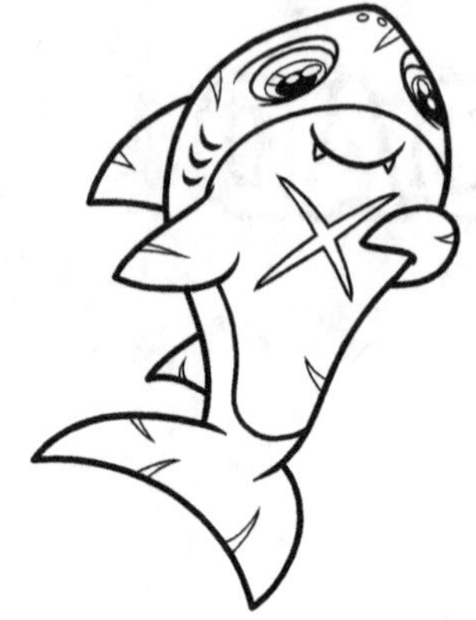

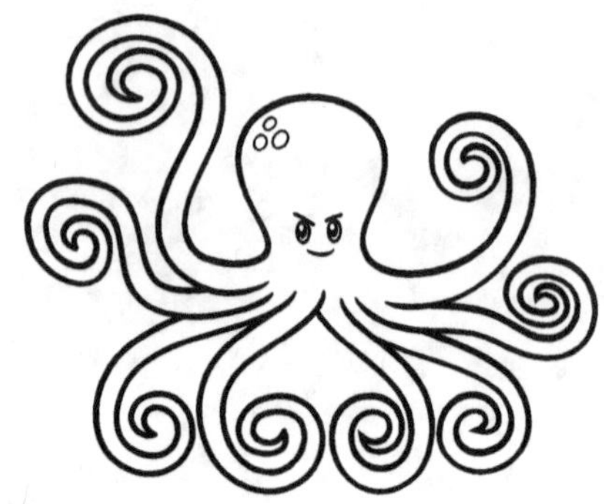

SEALIFE

COLORING BOOK

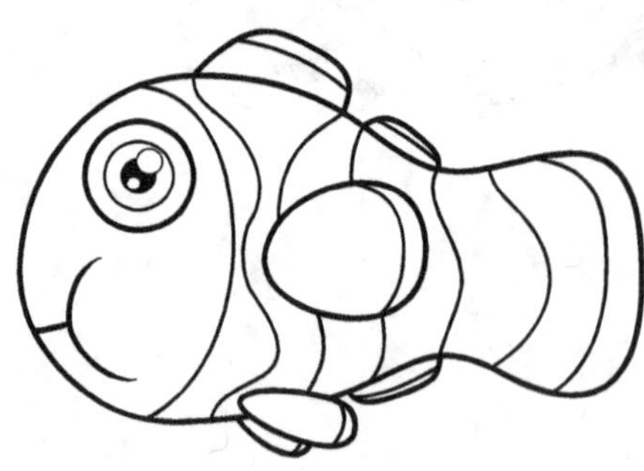

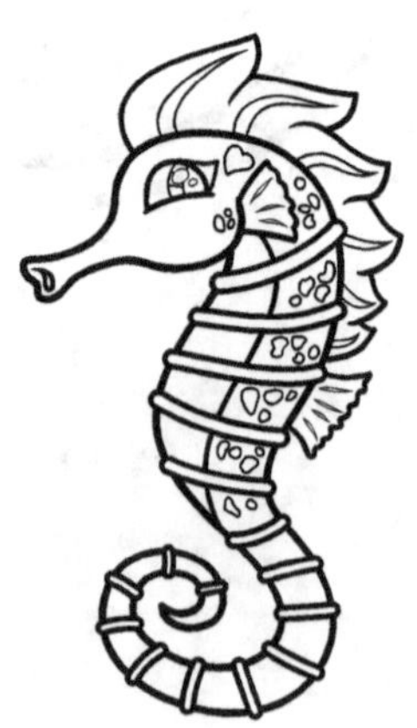

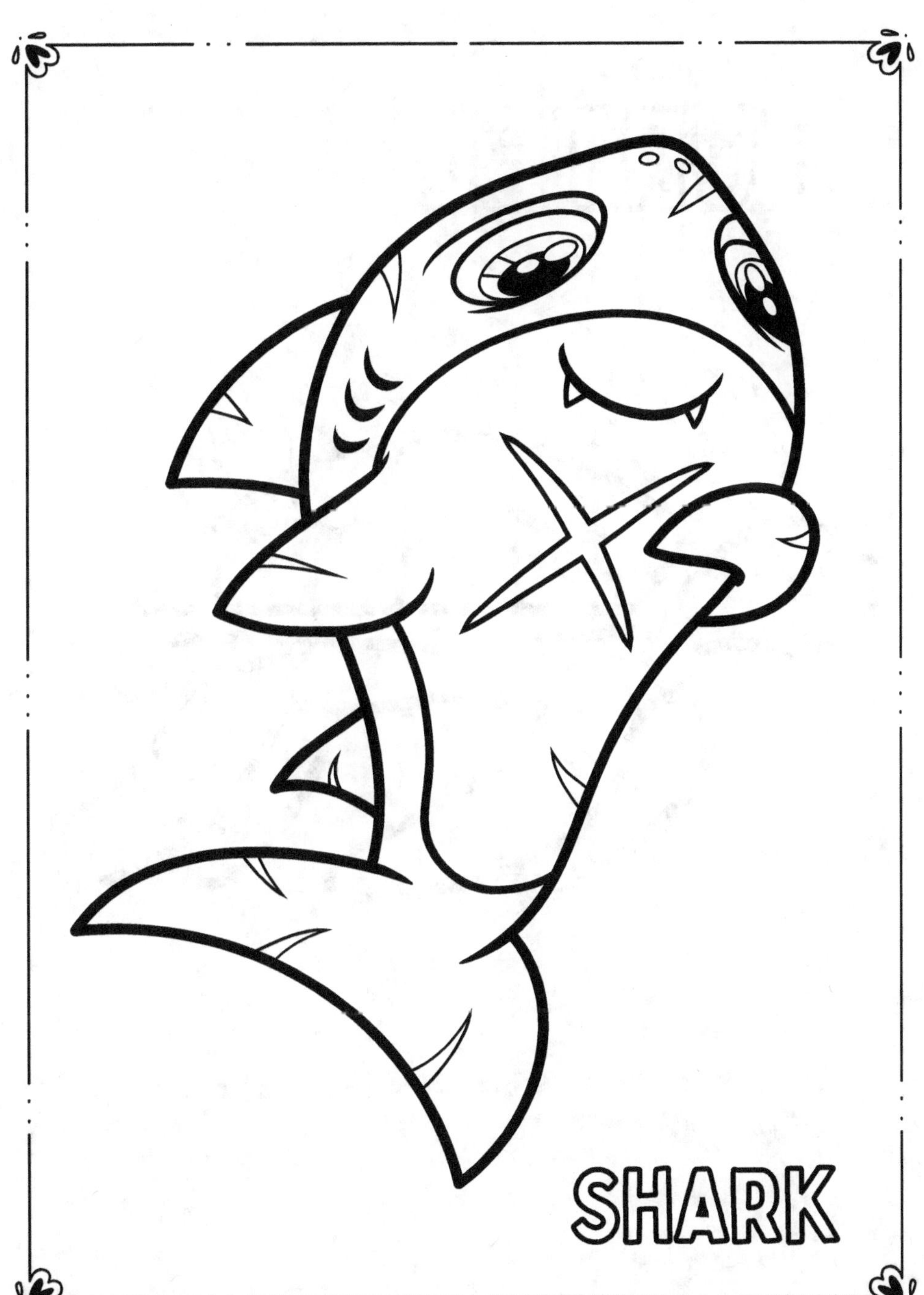
SHARK

TURTEL

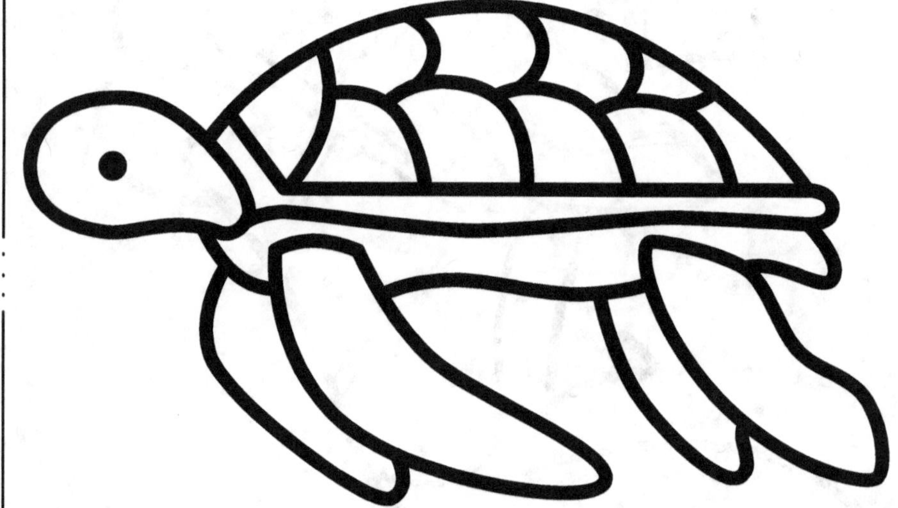

FISH

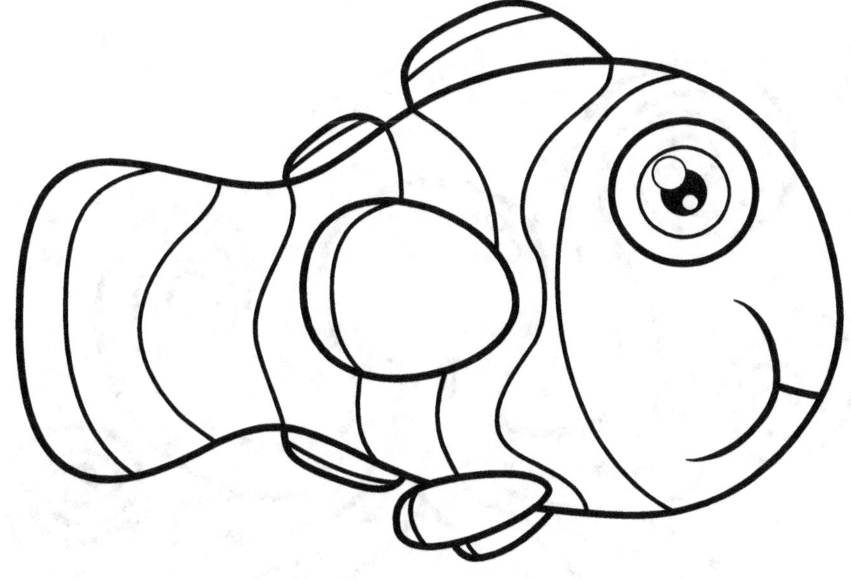

OCTOPUS

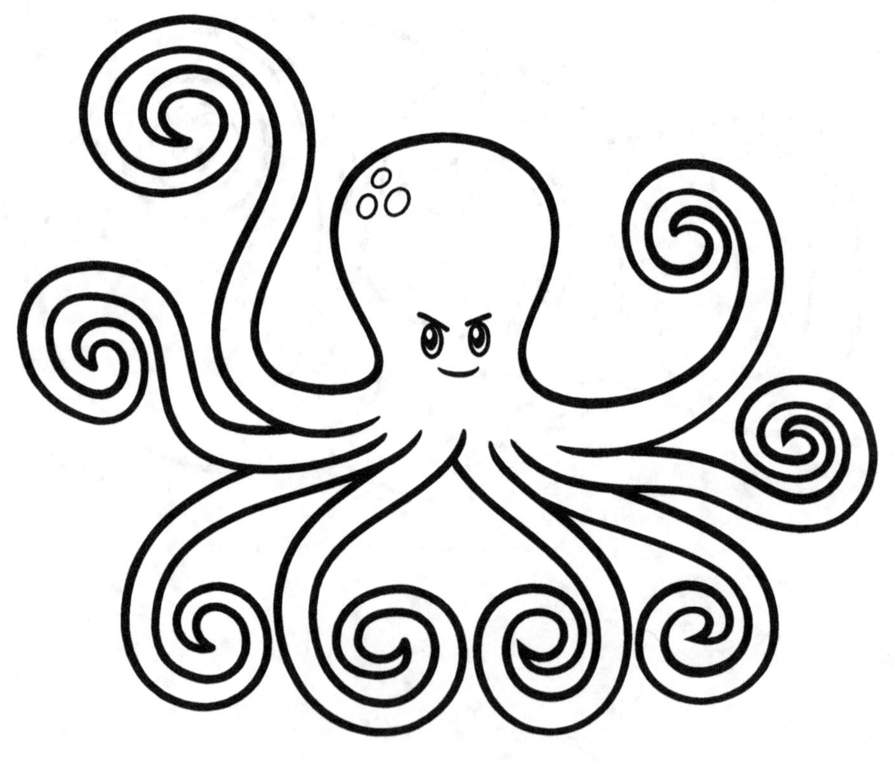

CRAB

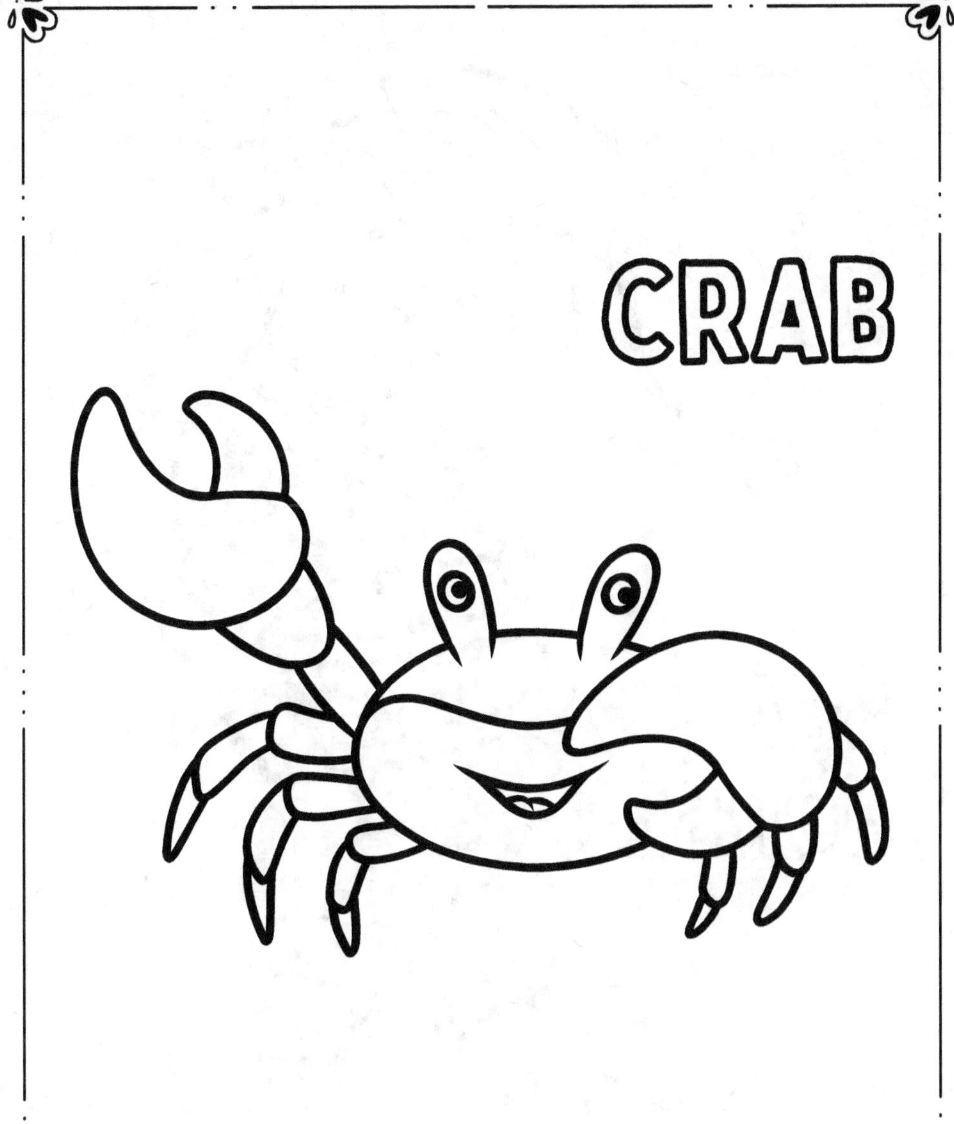

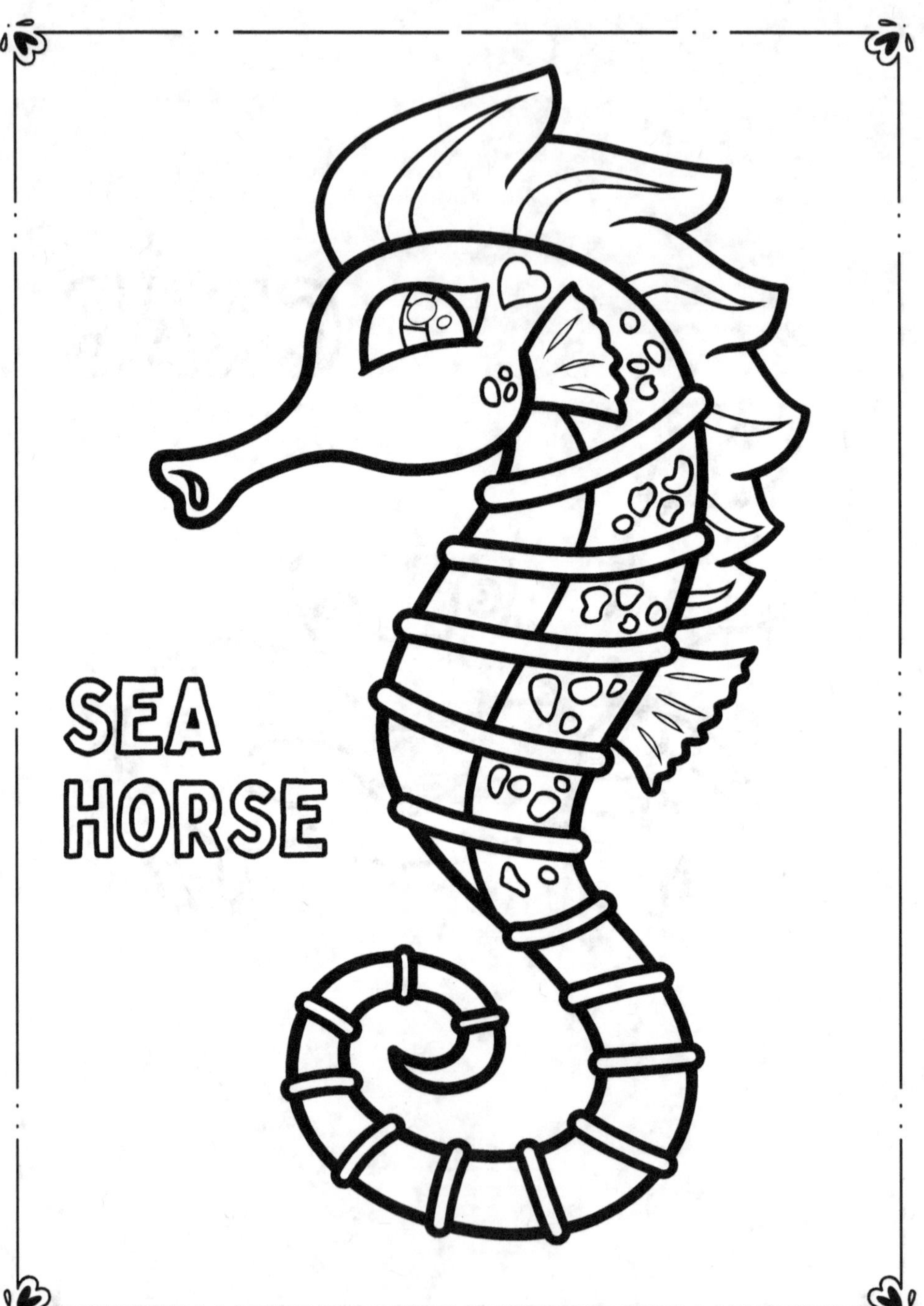

SEA
HORSE

SHELLFISH

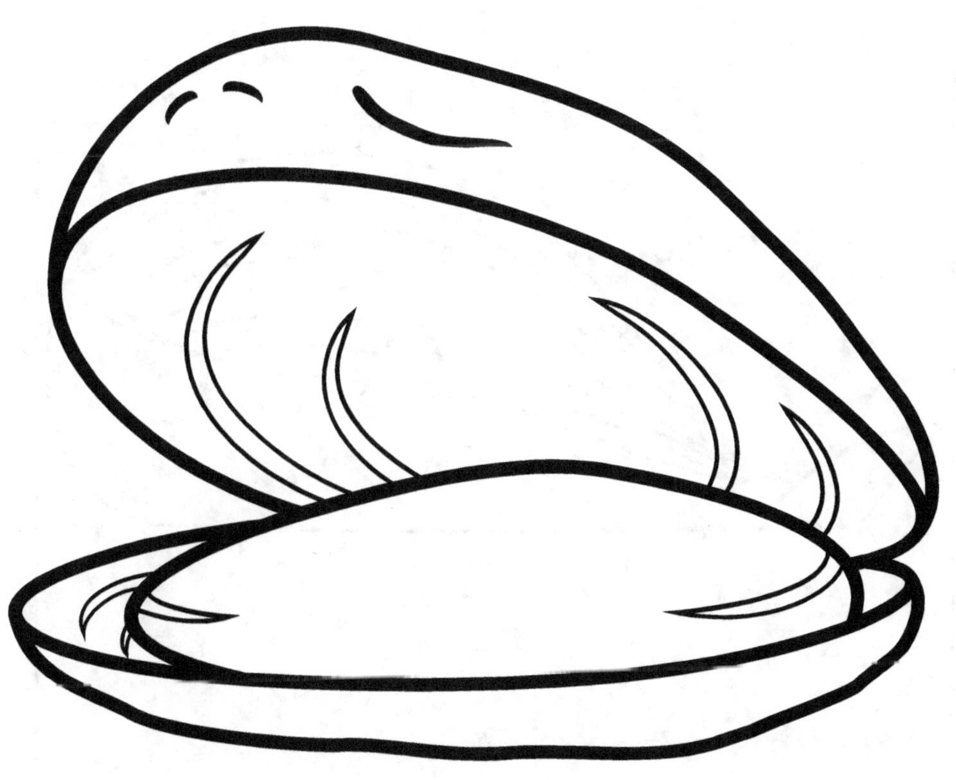

WHALE

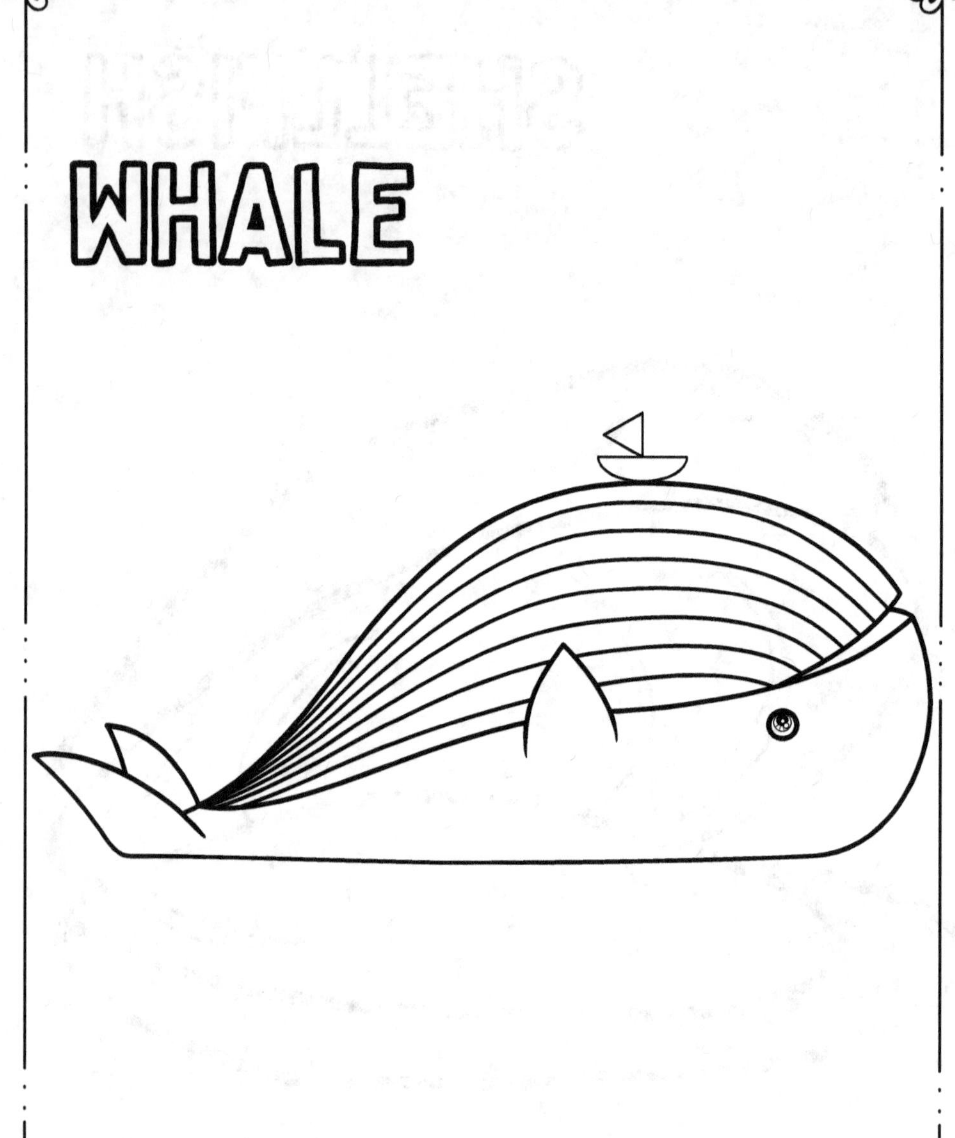

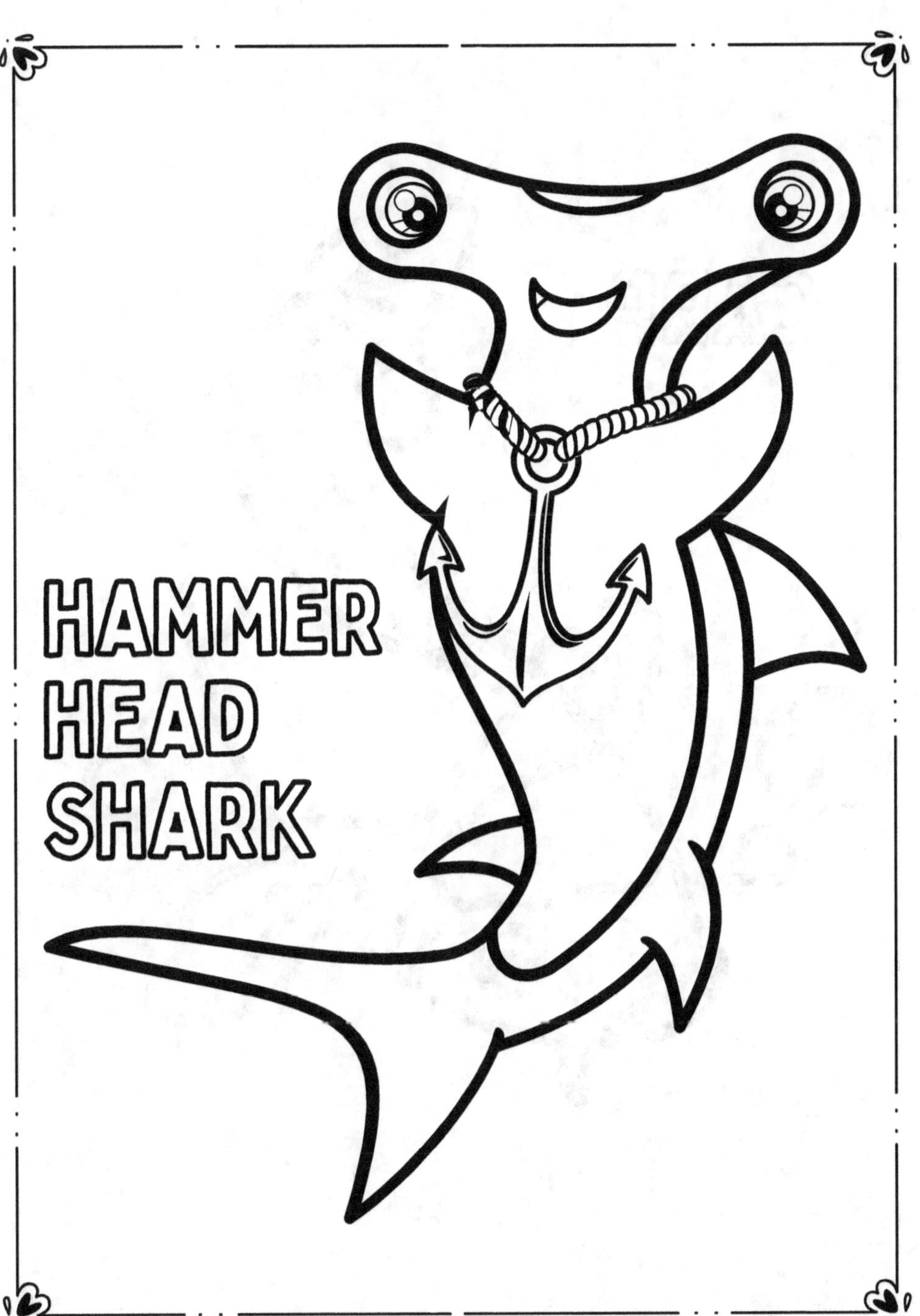

HAMMER HEAD SHARK

CARP

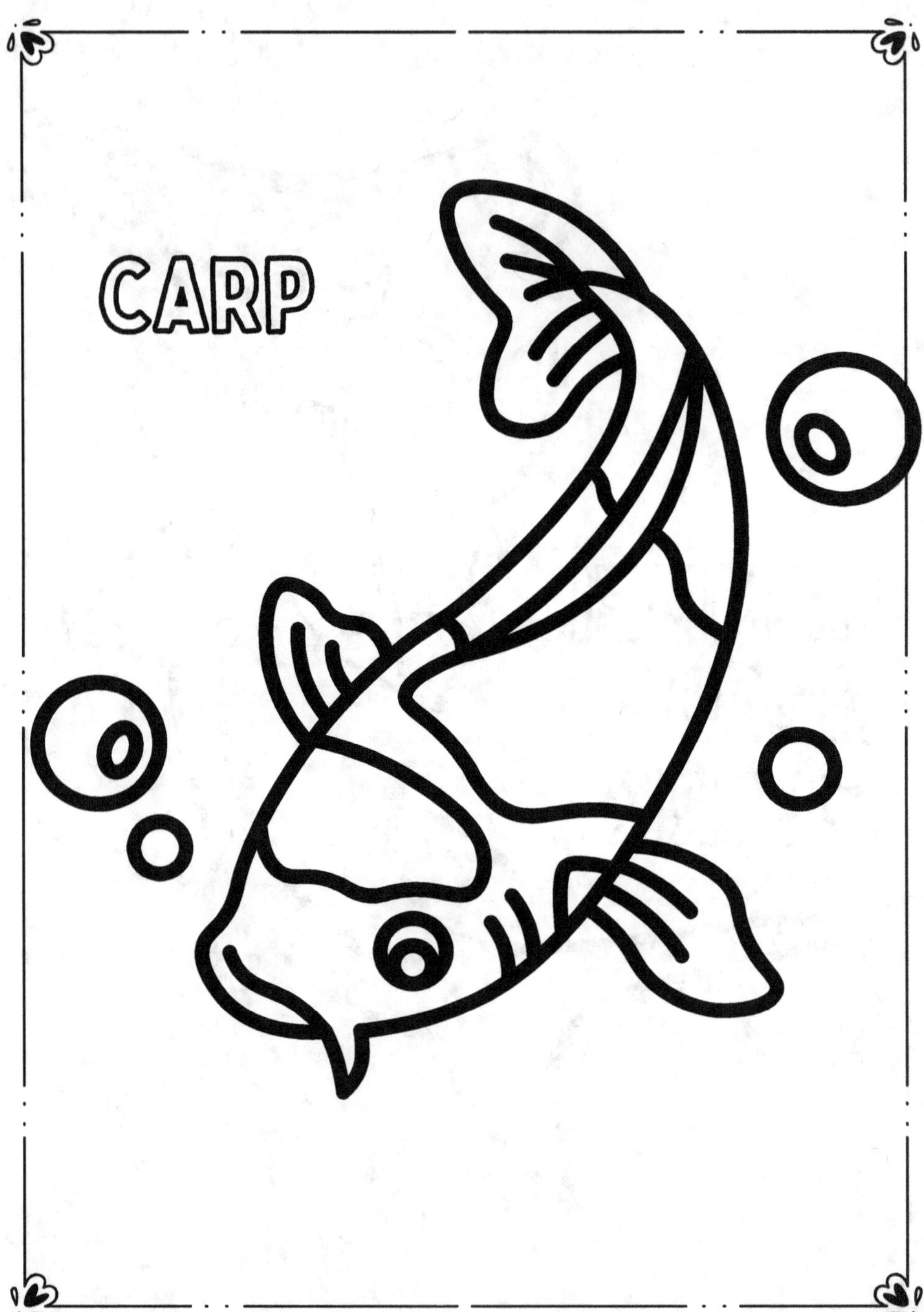

JELLYFISH

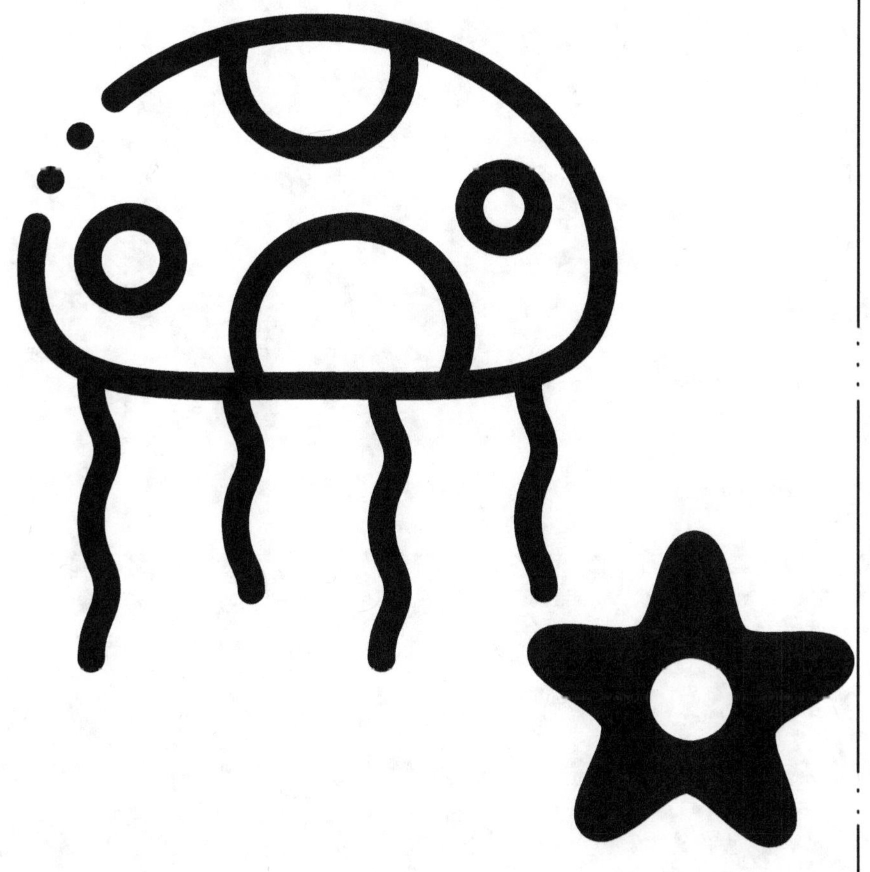